The Way of the Teacher

The Way of the Teacher

A Path for Personal Growth and Professional Fulfillment

Sandra Finney and Jane Thurgood Sagal

ROWMAN & LITTLEFIELD
Lanham • Boulder • New York • London

Published by Rowman & Littlefield
A wholly owned subsidiary of The Rowman & Littlefield Publishing Group, Inc.
4501 Forbes Boulevard, Suite 200, Lanham, Maryland 20706
www.rowman.com

Unit A, Whitacre Mews, 26-34 Stannary Street, London SE11 4AB

Copyright © 2017 by Sandra Finney and Jane Thurgood Sagal

All rights reserved. No part of this book may be reproduced in any form or by any electronic or mechanical means, including information storage and retrieval systems, without written permission from the publisher, except by a reviewer who may quote passages in a review.

British Library Cataloguing in Publication Information Available

Library of Congress Cataloging-in-Publication Data is Available

ISBN: 978-1-4758-3267-9 (cloth : alk. paper)
ISBN: 978-1-4758-3268-6 (pbk. : alk. paper)
ISBN: 978-1-4758-3269-3 (electronic)

∞™ The paper used in this publication meets the minimum requirements of American National Standard for Information Sciences—Permanence of Paper for Printed Library Materials, ANSI/NISO Z39.48-1992.

Printed in the United States of America

*For Jennifer Klenz, James Klenz, and all educators
who teach with compassion and commitment*

—Sandra Finney

*For Gareth Thurgood, Jeremy Thurgood, and Ksenia Thurgood
who inspired me to care for all students as valued children of the universe*

—Jane Thurgood Sagal

Contents

Preface		xi
Acknowledgments		xv
Introduction		1
PART I: TO KNOW THE SELF		**5**
1	A Way of Being	7
2	Understanding Our Essential Mystery	13
3	Remembering Our Purpose	17
4	Being Present	21
5	Honoring Our Suffering	27
6	Trusting Our Inner Knowledge	33
7	Practicing Self-compassion	39
8	Reflecting on Our Practice	45
PART II: TO IMBUE OUR CHALLENGES WITH HEART		**51**
9	Preserving Our Integrity	53
10	Working Well with Curriculum Requirements	57
11	Strengthening Our Resilience	63
12	Using Technology Wisely	69

13	Reducing Our Stress	75
14	Harmonizing Our Personal and Professional Lives	81
15	Creating Positive Energy in the Classroom	87
16	Writing Our Teaching Life	93

PART III: TO ENRICH AND DEEPEN OUR BEING — 99

17	Opening the Mind	101
18	Nurturing Our Love of Learning	107
19	Discovering the Beauty that Makes Us Whole	113
20	Bringing Forth Our Creativity	119
21	Finding Flow	123
22	Having a Hopeful Spirit	129
23	Increasing Happiness in Daily Life	135
24	Experiencing Joy	141

PART IV: TO STRENGTHEN OUR BONDS WITH OTHERS, AND THE NATURAL WORLD — 145

25	Teaching with Kindness	147
26	Keeping a Sense of Humour	153
27	Cultivating a Classroom Community	159
28	Supporting Teacher Voice	165
29	Sharing and Learning with Others	171
30	Seeking Nature, Outside and Indoors	177
31	Knowing the Earth Knows Us	181
32	Extending Kindness and Compassion to all Beings	185

Parting Thoughts	189
Appendix A: Mindfulness: A Short Primer	191
Appendix B: Negative Thoughts and Common Thinking Errors	197
Appendix C: Sample Personal-Professional Development Plans	201

Appendix D: Understanding Emotional and Spiritual Needs	205
Appendix E: How Connected to Nature Are You?	207
References	209
About the Authors	215

Preface

> Although people get paid to do their jobs, you cannot pay someone to do their job passionately and wholeheartedly. These qualities are not for sale; they are themselves gifts that can only be given freely. (Solnit, 2013, p. 120)

Teaching is demanding and rewarding work. Teaching becomes perhaps not less demanding, but certainly richer and more rewarding when we teach with passion, an open heart, and a genuine presence. These are qualities that can grow and become stronger and *The Way of the Teacher* looks at ways to support you in nurturing these dimensions of yourself and bringing forth more of what your heart, body, and mind already holds.

When we decided to write this book, we were nearing the end of long careers in education – ones that provided us with many perspectives on what it means to be a teacher and what kinds of teachers we most wanted to be. Whether from our experiences in a small country school, a public school in an affluent city neighborhood, from working as a senior administrator in a provincial education ministry, or as a professor in teacher education, the vision retained some essential qualities. The teachers we wanted for children and teenagers were ones with an authentic presence, joy in helping students learn, and a passion for learning themselves.

Experience upon experience taught us that who teachers are on the inside – the personal qualities they bring to the classroom – make the most difference in fostering the academic and personal growth of their students. As Kessler (2001) reminds us, "We can have the best curricula available, train teachers in technique and theory, but our students will be unsafe and our programs hollow if we do not provide opportunities for teachers to develop their own souls, their own social and emotional intelligence" (p. 118).

Seldom do teacher training courses, professional development offerings, or resources focus on the personal side of a teacher's development. Yet we found, and others confirmed, that personal development is the foundation of all other facets of professional[1] growth. There is an array of personal qualities and capabilities that make for inspiring, caring, and memorable teachers and *The Way of the Teacher* explores how these can be used and strengthened. The ideas, practices, and reflections in this book support this process.

At the center of personal development is self-knowledge – that knowledge and understanding which can deepen and mature through commitment and reflection and can be so essential to having an authentic presence in the classroom. *The Way of the Teacher* offers continuous opportunities for insight into the self, which reinvigorates the belief that students trust and value teachers who are genuine.

Cultivating an authentic presence is in many ways a stress-reducing process. It takes a lot of energy to maintain an image and act a role rather than be who we are. At the same time, the journey of self-knowledge never really ends; we evolve and change as teachers and can continue to become more of who we are – more creative, more compassionate, and more comfortable and natural in the classroom.

There are many ways to look at the essence of what a good teacher is and does and most of them converge on ideas of wholeness (i.e., a teacher who uses their mind, body, and heart, soul, or spirit[2]). The language for the part of us that feels deeply and senses more than is always visible doesn't matter so much as the recognition that it exists and helps to make us fully human. The book explores the inner life of the teacher using a non-religious framework and suggests ways to integrate the qualities and capabilities of body, mind, and heart or spirit into our teaching. While *The Way of the Teacher* works at several levels – from the practical and professional, to the personal and spiritual – it is the focus on inner qualities that promises to enrich your teaching life in sustaining ways.

Throughout, *The Way of the Teacher* describes a wide range of practices that help in the development of inner strength and wholeheartedness. The goal is to support your continued love of and joy in teaching, or to rekindle it through reflections and practices that cultivate self-knowledge and inner strength. Above all, the book's reflections and practices are designed to deepen your sense of what it means to be a teacher, help you bring your heart into your teaching life, and experience more ways to nourish your spirit.

AUDIENCE

While many individuals from different walks of life could find something useful in this book, it is to teachers and others related to the teaching profession that it speaks. The audience for the book includes both experienced and beginning teachers, school principals, student teachers, and professors of teacher education. It is designed to be used both by individuals and by teacher groups such as a school staff or a teacher book club. It is ideal for use in education classes and with teacher groups because the questions for reflection are designed to foster dialogue and deepen thinking. A strong point of the book is that the individual chapters are concise enough to be practical in the busy lives of teachers, yet with enough depth to be stimulating and thought-provoking.

PHILOSOPHY

The central metaphor of the book is that of a journey. The path is one of opening to the teaching life with a wise heart. You could also say the wise heart is the destination and that it is a destination that in a real way is always "here." Kabat-Zinn (2005) compares that sense of "here" to the way a discovery in science is always here even before it is seen, described, tested, and confirmed. He continues to illuminate the way a destination can always be ahead and at the same time always be here by comparing it to the process Michelangelo used when carving sculptures from a block of stone.

> He claimed that he merely removed what needed removing from a block of marble, revealing the figure that he "saw" with his own deep artist's eye, that was, in a sense, there from the beginning. Yet without real work, whatever might be here to be revealed in the domains of our own minds and hearts, even though it is already here, remains opaque and of no use to us. It is only "here" in its potentiality. For it to be revealed requires us to participate in a process of possible revelation, and to be willing to be shaped and transmuted in turn by the process itself. (pp. 97–98)

The philosophy of the book is that as you work with the ideas, you bring forth what is already within you so the journey is one of helping you find or remember the knowledge and gifts you contain. We hope your appreciation of who you are and of the richness of possibilities the teaching life offers will grow as you walk The Way of the Teacher.

NOTES

1. See for example, the work of Caine and Caine (2010), Kessler (2001) and Palmer (1998).

2. We use *heart, spirit,* and *soul* in this book to refer to the core of our being – that which integrates our feelings, thoughts, and highest values, gives life more meaning, and leads to a greater sense of connection to all of life.

Acknowledgments

The authors gratefully acknowledge the dedicated time spent by and insightful feedback received from reviewers with a variety of educational backgrounds and experiences. The comments and ideas we received helped to ensure our language, ideas, and suggestions were well grounded in practice and supported deep reflections about the teaching life. Our many thanks to:

Sue Amundrud, Teaching for Understanding coach, WIDE World (Widescale Interactive Development for Educators), Harvard Graduate School of Education

Karen Bedford, former primary teacher, Nipissing School Board, North Bay ON

Charla Jo Guillaume, social studies teacher, Memorial Composite High School, Parkland School Division #70, Stony Plain AB

Mandy Ish, graduate student, College of Education, University of Saskatchewan

Samantha Mirwarld, learning support facilitator, Prairie Spirit School Division, Warman SK

Patricia Peech, speech pathologist and learning resource support facilitator, Prairie Spirit School Division, Warman SK

Rae Porter, former elementary school teacher, Saskatchewan school divisions, Kelvington and Regina SK

Dennis Schaefer, music educator and former curriculum developer for Arts Education, Saskatchewan Ministry of Education

Dianne Warren, author and former curriculum developer for Arts Education, Saskatchewan Ministry of Education

Colleen Watson Turner, artist and former teacher, Saskatoon Public School Division

Sharon Yuzdepski, former curriculum director, Saskatchewan Ministry of Education

Introduction

> Personal transformation comes first. It is the most important work. If you can't choose hope and optimism, you can't expect that of others. . . . You cannot help others create what you cannot create yourself. (Showkeir & Showkeir, 2008, p. 79)

Teaching is a creative endeavor that draws on the full range of our human abilities – emotional, physical, social, intellectual, and spiritual. No matter what age group or which subjects you teach, there are many needs to be met. Your students need you to be clear and organized, kind, patient, and trustworthy. Administrators need you to be all these things, and to follow prescribed curricula and comply with the regulations of the larger institution. Parents and the public want you to be accountable for student learning but have many different ideas about what that accountability should look like. You want to meet these needs and challenges in a way that brings you satisfaction and fulfillment. *The Way of the Teacher* is a resource to support you in living your vision of the good teacher and in growing as a person through your teaching – developing inner strength and insight, with moments of joy along the way.

To sustain a wholehearted teaching practice in the face of its challenges, our teaching needs to come from a deeper source – one that strengthens our sense of connection to our students, our colleagues, and our inner life. Whether referred to as the spirit, the soul, or the heart, it is a source of vitality, emotional courage, and compassion. Spiritual strength gives us greater presence and passion, the means to recover from sorrows and setbacks, and more ways to experience small pleasures and moments of insight and recognition.

Cultivation of the soul helps us develop an appreciation for beauty, for the mysteries of existence, and opens up more sources of meaning for us. Listening to the heart brings us knowledge not available in any other way. Spiritual strength and wholeheartedness bring an "aliveness" to our school life, a vitality, a steadiness, and a ready joy in the learning and happiness of our students.

To teach well, we need to understand the links between personal and professional growth.

One way to illuminate these links, which is also the book's approach to teacher wholeness, is to look at a challenge such as implementing a new curriculum or program and asking what personal qualities are needed to meet this challenge well or what virtues support this task. The book answers these questions through paying attention to body, mind, and spirit or heart and examining such things as:

- how the body can help us, such as, through using all the senses or noticing muscle tension
- how the heart can help us through drawing on our kindness
- how the spirit can support us through giving us courage
- how the mind supports us in reflecting on what thoughts are helpful in particular situations and in recognizing relationships.

The book incorporates all these sources of support but gives particular attention to the knowledge and abilities that come from the heart, spirit, and soul.

Textbox I.1 shows examples of personal qualities, virtues, and values that are emphasized throughout the book and that enable teachers in becoming strong, effective, and wholehearted. Often, qualities and virtues overlap and can be looked at from either perspective.

The Way of the Teacher is organized to support our wholeness through increasing our self-knowledge, imbuing our challenges with heart, deepening our being, and strengthening our bonds with others.

These are the themes that organize the book into four parts. Each part contains eight chapters with each chapter focused on a central aspect of personal

---

Textbox I.1 Personal Qualities and Virtues that Sustain and Enrich the Teaching Life

Personal Qualities: Genuine, Natural, Self-Knowledge, Present and Aware, Open, Kind/Caring, Fair, Good-humored, Modest, Creative, Truthful, Trustworthy, Enthusiastic, Clear, Patient, Respectful, Friendly, Dependable, Compassionate, Collegial, Cooperative, Imaginative, Understanding, Encouraging, Happy, Relaxed, At Ease, Nonthreatening

Virtues & Values: Forgiveness, Moral Courage, Humility, Hope, Wisdom, Honesty, Dignity, Equanimity, Perseverance, Beauty, Vitality, Moderation, Sensitivity, Peace

development and the teaching life. The personal qualities or virtues supported in each chapter are ones research affirms as those most necessary to teach well, inspire and care for our students, continue to nurture our own love of learning, and grow as a person and a teacher.[1]

The design of the book is such that you can focus on one part at a time exploring the chapters sequentially, or use the chapters in whatever order appears most meaningful for the individuals or teacher groups who are using it for personal-professional development.

The chapters in *The Way of the Teacher* are based on research – that which has stood the tests of time and new findings. For example, the book includes insights from the growing field of positive psychology in which research has discovered consistent sources of happiness and a variety of means to a happier life. All works that have been used in the content of the chapters are included in the reference list.

Key themes in the book surface in several chapters, each time from a slightly different perspective. In this sense, some overlap in the Questions and Practices is intentional. Quotes have been chosen to open each chapter, some from non-fiction works and others from fiction. This is intended to illustrate different ways that humans can understand their lives and to provide different kinds of perspectives in relation to a topic. Most chapters contain teachers' anecdotes. They are included to make connections between central ideas in the chapter and the realities of classroom life. These stories are in italics to set them apart from other quoted materials.

All of the chapters are designed to support reflection through the inclusion of a section called *Some Questions to Ask*. The questions are intended to foster further thinking, promote discussion, and generate other questions. Each chapter also includes a section called *Some Practices to Consider*, which suggests a range of possibilities you could incorporate in relation to the chapter's focus. These practices are not meant to be a list of more things to do. Rather, they are intended to capture aspects of the chapter's themes that you can choose from and integrate into your daily practice or personal life to develop inner strength and greater joy. The *Questions* and *Practices* are intended to be used by both individuals and groups. Their wording alternates between "we" and "I" to reflect both possibilities. All chapters conclude with *Thoughts to Remember* – a short summary of its major ideas.

Part I begins the work of personal growth through ideas and practices that strengthen self-knowledge and care for the spirit. Particularly important in this foundation of knowing the self is reflection – asking the questions that illuminate our experiences, our wishes and worries, dreams and commitments. Each chapter in Part One provides the material that sparks deep reflection and makes the achievement of greater self-knowledge and a strong spirit possible.

Part II examines the challenges of teaching through the lens of head and heart wisdom. You will find perspectives on teacher resilience, stress reduction, preserving integrity and other commonplaces of the teaching life by starting from the sense of teaching as a way of listening deeply, observing with kindness, and teaching with care for our students and the subject matter under study.

Part III of the book explores all the ways we can enrich our life by further developing these inner dimensions of our being. The chapters describe ways to increase open-mindedness, love of learning, creativity, and deep engagement through finding flow. Part III culminates with a focus on practices that support us in maintaining a hopeful orientation, and experiencing greater happiness and joy.

A strong and open heart helps us to feel a profound sense of connection to life – to all people, the natural world, and our own inner life. Part IV explores how important it is to feel this strong sense of connection and care for our students, colleagues, and other humans and for the natural world and all it contains. It contains many ideas for strengthening our bonds and deepening our understanding of the ways in which everything on Earth is interconnected and contributes to the whole.

NOTE

1. See for example the work of Freeman and Scheidecker (2009) and Stronge, Tucker, and Hindman (2004).

Part I

TO KNOW THE SELF

Know Thyself is its own end and has no end. . . . There is no other end than the end of soul-making itself and soul is without end.[1]

NOTE

1. Hillman, J. (1983). *Healing Fiction.* Woodstock, NY: Spring Publications, pp. 47–49.

Chapter 1

A Way of Being

> Our way of being in the world of the classroom – whether we are "being peace" or "being impatience," "being respect" or "being condescension," "being awareness" or "being numb" – will ultimately determine how safe and open students will feel when we invite them to explore deep matters. Students are very sensitive to the qualities of their guides. (Kessler, 2001, p. 118)

Teaching involves so many actions, yet it is the teacher's way of being that ultimately colors these actions for better or worse and affects students' learning and growth. When we say that, as a teacher, it is important not just *what* you do but the *way* you do it, we are talking about the personal qualities that people bring to their teaching. A way of being with students and with the learning process can be genuine and enthusiastic; thoughtful and encouraging of students' questions; shallow or lacking in authenticity; kind but anxious; tolerant of some ambiguity or needing conformity and control.

Our way of being is colored by social and cultural factors such as our ethnicity, economic circumstances, and first language. This is also the case for our students. To respond well to the intellectual, physical, social, cultural, and economic diversity of our students, we need to be aware of how *we* have been shaped and of our attitudes to human differences. When we are open to responding thoughtfully, we can seek professional support such as workshops and learn from our students and their families about their ways of being and the values they hold. This can be a mutually enriching practice.

We may be quite unaware of what we are conveying to students through our body language, tone of voice, and the degree to which we are able to encourage and listen to students' ideas. We might not notice that we have a tendency to support some students but neglect others or where this pattern comes from. Increasing our awareness of what type of presence we have in the classroom is an important step toward greater authenticity. Whether recognized or not, our teaching flows from the quality of our inner life.

> *Margie was a dear little girl, a bright-eyed, lively, and spirited being. She came to school each day full of cheer and mischief. I was drawn to her as an original being and exasperated by her intractability. She could not stay in her desk or at a table. She was in constant motion, taking someone's pencil, teasing a classmate, completing few tasks, but always smiling. I did not understand what she needed and I think now that I didn't ask that question enough or sufficiently deeply.*
>
> *Without understanding the meaning her behaviours might have, I often asked her to take her work and sit in the cloakroom and to come out again when she felt ready to be part of the class without bothering others. I thought my way of lessening her strain on her classmates was better than harsh words and, at the time, I guess I didn't understand isolation as a wound to the spirit.*
>
> *The irony of this practice was made clear to me by another teacher who came to observe my classroom and the way I used a play-based approach to working with grade one students. Visiting teachers were asked to write comments about what they observed and one teacher wrote, "I just feel sorry for Margie. She seems to be out of the classroom activities more than she's in." This shocked me and still hurts when I think of it – not because it offended me but because I had to face how I was harming Margie. How was it that I, who had a genuine concern for the well-being of the children, could be unaware of what isolation might be really teaching a child? What might I have done to engage Margie in the learning activities for longer periods of time?*

These types of questions cause us to reach both inward and outward – inward to greater self-understanding and outward to the realm of best practices for fostering student engagement. We believe that knowing the self is a necessary and important path for understanding our students, what their needs are, and how they are feeling. It is this foundation of self-knowledge that supports learning and creates classroom climate.

Part of our journey to greater understanding of our classroom presence is an exploration of what kind of teacher we mean to be. What qualities make a person a teacher? What does it mean to be a teacher in the most profound sense of the word? Taking some time to explore the heart of what it means to "teach" will help us in assessing if our way of being in the classroom matches our vision of what a teacher is and does. This is a foundation for becoming more aware of our instructional tendencies and predominant ways of responding to students.

Teachers at their best have the gift of drawing new knowledge, abilities, and moral and aesthetic qualities out of those who spend time with them. Such a teacher leaves others better in some way – kinder, stronger, more open, and ultimately more prepared to learn from what life offers. This preparation is accompanied by the sense that life is meaningful. A teacher enlivens the other, lights their imagination and often also touches their heart. The height and depth of this vision is not so much attained as worked toward and can be used for reflecting on how we are now and how this shapes the way we teach.

It strengthens our self-awareness to understand that teaching takes place in many settings including a classroom, a home, an office, or the outdoors. In a lifetime, we may have many teachers, sometimes a child, sometimes an elder, a poet, a carpenter, a dog, a tree, a flower. Each person and element of the teaching-learning relationship influences the others. Sometimes the teacher-student relationship is reversed – the teacher learns, the student informs or inspires. In the classroom setting, a teacher's self-knowledge is a large part of what students sense as authenticity. The degree to which teachers recognize and understand their own feelings influences the extent to which they really see and hear their students as persons with ideas to express and needs to meet.

Self-knowledge grows not only from reflection on our own life but also from knowing the range of experiences that others undergo, from suffering to joy, compassion to cruelty. The recognition that some children are emotionally, physically, or sexually abused and that these forms of suffering might be a part of any home is essential for teachers. Learning that the educational and income levels of parents are not an indicator that children are safe and protected can break through a teacher's naïveté and foster a deeper understanding of the human predicament. These can be hard realities for teachers to face; but with the pain we feel in the face of a child's suffering comes greater compassion and a stronger ability to understand the needs that affect a student's learning.

Many teachers realize when they look back on their experiences as young teachers that they have often been naive and unaware of the ways they had been shaped that may have hampered their own growth. This lack of awareness sometimes meant not seeing the gifts, interests, or the suffering of their students. We might have been well-meaning but might have followed many accepted practices without necessarily questioning if there were stronger ways to create an atmosphere that supported learning and at the same time, matched who we were as persons. Experience, coupled with kindness toward ourselves, and the intention to continue to grow as teachers and as persons, can help us become more natural.

This journey from good intentions to a more grounded understanding and mature and compassionate way of being has at its heart what all teachers possess – the desire to learn more as a scholar, and deepen and grow as a human. The vision of what it means to be a true teacher develops and changes with self-understanding. As one teacher put it,

I came to have a sense of compassion for myself as my humanness came into view, and I finally began to reclaim and "remember" my mind, body, and soul. A practice that puts us back in touch with our own soul is the foundation necessary for touching the souls of others. Thich Nhat Hanh reflects this when saying: "Caring for yourself, re-establishing peace in yourself is the basic condition for helping someone else." (Caldwell, 2011, p. 101)

Some Questions to Ask Are:

- What do I mean when I say someone is a teacher? How do I exemplify this vision?
- What do I think children and teenagers need in order to do their best learning? How do I respond to these needs through my way of being in the classroom?
- Am I comfortable with turning inward to better understand my own feelings and needs?
- Do I feel at ease in my teaching and able to be myself, yet professional?
- To what extent do we feel that our way of being in the classroom is authentic and unique to us and in what ways is it a reflection of conventional teachers' roles we might have imbibed from our own teachers or during teacher education? Can our way of being come from both inner and outer sources?

Some Practices to Consider Are:

- Allow yourself time to grow and learn as a teacher and as a human. Use the understanding that teaching is a rich and complex endeavor, a web of relationships, an art and a practice that is never fully mastered, to be gentle with yourself on the path of personal and professional growth.
- Try to learn something about yourself from your students with each class that you teach. The insights might come from a lesson, a day, or reflecting back on a year or semester.
- Dialogue groups: Share ideas about what particular ways of being in the classroom might look, sound, and feel like and how each teacher has a unique presence. Set the intention to notice how your way of being in the world affects your students and dedicate your next meeting to discussing and reflecting on this focus.

Thoughts to Remember

The qualities that a teacher brings to teaching influence the classroom atmosphere and the quality and degree of student learning. The journey to become authentic and comfortable with oneself involves working toward greater self-understanding and a willingness to grow and change. One way to increase knowledge of our own qualities is to reflect deeply on our ideas of what it means to be a teacher – one that leaves students better in meaningful ways from spending a term or a year with us. Then we can compare our vision with our knowledge of our own social, emotional, and spiritual gifts to assess which areas of personal growth we want to strengthen.

It is helpful to remember that children and teenagers desire authentic connection with us. Greater self-understanding helps us to really see and hear our students – recognizing their needs and respecting their ideas.

Chapter 2

Understanding Our Essential Mystery

> The stars, Earth, stones, life of all kinds, form a whole in relation to each other and so close is this relationship that we cannot understand a stone without some understanding of the great sun. No matter what we touch, an atom or a cell, we cannot explain it without knowledge of the universe. The laws governing the universe can be made interesting and wonderful to children, more interesting than things in themselves, and they begin to ask: What am I? What is the task of humanity in this wonderful universe? (Maria Montessori, as quoted in Suzuki, 2007, pp. 22–23)

It is not only children who ask the question, "Who am I?" It is a life question, an adventure of discovery. Our essential mystery cannot be fully penetrated. To describe this knowledge as a mystery, we mean that each of us has a unique and marvelous essence that is ours alone and that core of what makes us unique cannot be fully known.

This mystery is three-fold. The first aspect of the mystery of human existence is that no two humans are the same – human diversity is infinite. Dr. Seuss has some wonderful lines that celebrate the uniqueness of each of us. In one of his books he says, "Today you are You, that is truer than true. There is no one alive who is Youer than You."

The second form of mystery is that even *we* don't know everything about ourselves and we never will no matter how much self-knowledge we have. There is always more to learn. We learn and grow and change and, as Montessori observed, we are so interconnected with the people and the life forms and forces around us that we are continuously influenced by them – often in unpredictable ways. It helps to see that we are never finished with learning, growing, and changing and also to question more deeply just what we mean by the self. We may see that self-making is a creative process. As Brian Swimme (2001) puts it, "You are not just the things you do, not just the thoughts you think, the convictions you hold. You are a power creating the whole complex work of art that is your life, your manifestation in the world" (p. 129).

The third and profound aspect of the mystery of humanness is that there is a deep and essential shaping of our being – the heart of who we are, which can be sensed but is never fully revealed. Humans across time and from all cultures have recognized this precious innerness that we call our spirit and our soul.

This means we can ask the question, "Who am I?" at many levels. One place to start might be to look at our roles and see ourselves as a teacher, a parent, a mate, a daughter or son, a friend, an athlete, an artist, or any other roles we play. We can extend this to look at our gifts, our interests, beliefs, challenges, joys, fears, and dreams and discover more about ourselves. Still, there is more – there are parts of us as yet undiscovered, parts of us that are changing, growing, and deepening. Rosenbaum (2013) describes humans as beings in nonstop flow and says, "The real you does not stop or start but whirls and streams" (p. 7).

This is the mystery of transcendence. We can imagine and dream and create, and sometimes these abilities are the fuel that leads to gaining new strength, overcoming past difficulties and habits, and becoming more than we were. Artist, poet, and philosopher M.C. Richards (1989) describes this "more" when she says, "We carry light within us" (p. 18). We have a spirit that seeks to connect with all that is, a heart that can endlessly open, a soul that seeks depth, and a mind that seeks wisdom. These longings and transformations are always possible and know no bounds. We are always changing, growing, and becoming. Richo (2005) suggests the human soul, like the universe, is infinite.

A way of being, that acknowledges the spirit, recognizes other life forms and natural settings as sacred and worthy of protection and respect. The sense of coming out of ourselves to merge with the living things around us can be deeply restorative and a capacity of the spirit which we all have.

Whether or not we hold a view of the soul or spirit from a particular religious or spiritual tradition or allow for the mystery of the unbounded self from a secular perspective, our life is enriched by the appreciation that to be fully human is to be more than a mind in a body. Paul Houston, a greatly respected educator and leader, who has co-authored books on the spiritual dimension of education and given many workshops and presentations says,

> When I talk about spirituality, I am talking about those things that bring us together as humans. To me, spirituality is simply creating a deeper connection to our most profound human aspects. It is also a willingness to reach out to others and join in the human dance that unites us. And it is the desire to strengthen that

golden cord that connects us to our own version of the divine. A leader who is in touch with these concepts will be able to affect others in the organization to be open to them as well. And when the adults are open, the children can walk through the gate. (2011, p. ix)

When you understand yourself as a sacred being, you can also hold your students in this same deeply respectful way.

Some Questions to Ask Are:

- Do I see myself, my students, and my colleagues as sacred beings worthy of being treated unconditionally with dignity and respect? In what ways does this shape how I interact with them?
- Do I sometimes surprise myself by what I say and do?
- Do I recognize the ways by which I have transcended past selves to become stronger, more creative, or compassionate?
- Are there times in my life when I sense the mysteries of existence, when I sense that there is something more to life than can be captured in words? Do I sense this mystery and "more" in myself and in my teaching?
- Does it change how we teach and relate to others when we acknowledge that there are aspects of life and ourselves that contain mystery, which cannot be fully known? Do we see these aspects of mystery as being connected with the spirit, soul, or the sacred?

Some Practices to Consider Are:

- Use a reflection on what the concepts of soul, spirit, and the human heart mean to you and how they describe aspects of yourself that can't be fully known yet enlarge the dimensions of your being for journal writing or conversation with a friend.
- Find ways to support student explorations of the great questions of existence such as, "Why am I here and what is my role in the universe?" Ensure that these explorations are respectful of all cultures and religious and spiritual practices.
- Dialogue groups: Seek out books and workshops that explore the spiritual dimension of teaching and learning and share insights from these. Use some of the questions above to support group dialogue.

Thoughts to Remember

It is a strengthening and compelling practice to reflect on the mystery of who we are from our outward appearance and personal characteristics to the very essence of our being. Whether we have a religious community and a relationship to the Divine or live within a secular framework, the spirit or heart calls to us and we can feel this whether or not we can articulate it. Holding a view of the soul, the spirit, and the sacred in whatever way we can feeds and supports our life and draws us into respectful and caring relationships with others and the earth.

You do not need to teach this directly to your students to help them to see that they contain mystery and more love and strength than they might think. The way in which you see your students as unique and precious beings changes the atmosphere of the classroom and supports your students in feeling emotionally safe – safe to question, safe to learn, safe to grow, and safe to love. This, in turn, supports you to continue to reflect on your essential mystery.

Chapter 3

Remembering Our Purpose

> [Teachers] are active agents whose words and deeds change lives and mold futures. . . . Given how difficult it is to be a teacher, I've become increasingly interested in why teachers stay in teaching, particularly excellent and caring teachers of diverse backgrounds and students challenged by poverty, racism, and injustice. It is clear to me that such teachers are often at the center of student success. Through their daily practice, they play a key role in upholding the ideal of equal and high quality education. (Nieto, 2003, pp. 19–20)

Sonia Nieto's extensive experience in working with students with challenges of language, ethnicity, and poverty and her research into what keeps teachers going in tough situations demonstrate that while teachers are not the only factor in students' success, they are the most crucial factor. Their dedication to their students comes from their values, beliefs, their own experiences, and above all their desire to make a positive difference in the lives of those they teach. For the majority of teachers, the decision to become a teacher is a decision to contribute in some way to a better world.

This sense of purpose already confirms your goodness and reveals that you care about young people and the quality of their lives. Teachers who find their work to be fulfilling believe that they are contributing to a greater good and they tend to view their work as a "calling" or end in itself that gives their life meaning and purpose. Thomas Moore (2008) talks about work in relation to what it offers the soul when your work comes from a deep sense of who you are.

> To be open to soul means to be open to the life that pools deep inside you, allowing it to coalesce into a career or other kind of work. Your choice of work flows from who you are – from your interests, tastes, hopes, and values. As you work, you feel that you are doing something consonant with your nature. (p. 28)

Palmer (2000) calls this principle "letting your life speak," meaning listening to our heart to find the work and the vision that truly fit who we are and what we care most about. From his many years in counseling, Moore (2008) concludes that much of the stress people feel in work is owing to the absence of love (i.e., not being fully and deeply engaged in work that is felt to be valuable both for the ways it makes the lives of others better and because it is a source of true satisfaction and moments of joy). The fact that you have been drawn to teaching suggests that you are seeking to contribute to a higher good. Revisiting what that good is which you wish to achieve with your teaching can help you to rededicate and renew your motivation to achieving it.

To hear a call, we begin by listening. In the case of finding our vocation as a teacher, we need to first listen deeply to our heart and what it is telling us about who we are and what we are meant to do. We must listen for the values at the center of our own identity and not choose teaching because others have said this is what we should do. As teachers we need to be authentic first, and the purposes we wish to fulfill must be our own. We recognize our dreams of contributing to students' lives through our teaching as genuine when they evoke a sense of gladness in our hearts.

It seems important to note here that many of us started out with very simple reasons for choosing teaching. An example might be that we enjoyed mathematics and thought we could do a good job teaching it. This is a good starting point. We can broaden this sense of calling gradually as we experience the full potential of the teaching role. This process is one of enlarging our teaching purposes to include our highest values. For many people in the helping professions, this highest value is a commitment to become more loving. Richo (2005) says this commitment makes us stronger emotionally and spiritually.

> Our universal calling as humans is to be the most loving people we can be. This commitment makes us less likely to be at the mercy of others' reactions to us or opinions of us. We appreciate acceptance but do not crave or cling to it. We are hurt by rejection but not devastated by it. Our focus is on how we love, not on how we are loved, on how we can give, not on what we can get. What a loss to the world it would be if we lived our lives and neglected to activate fully our wondrously wide capacity to love! (p. 27)

The more we can align our daily lessons and interactions with our larger purpose, the more likely we are to find our teaching fulfilling and motivating.[1] Our students also have ideas about meaning and purpose, and appreciate opportunities to reflect on how they might contribute to a better world. Supporting this focus with them through practices such as personal writing, dialogue groups, and Sharing Circles[2] can be inspiring as we witness their idealism and passion for contributing to a better world. This is a meaningful way to strengthen our own sense of purpose.

> *As I matured in my teaching practice, I found myself focusing more often on giving students opportunities to explore questions of meaning and purpose. I always preferred to use Remembrance Day assemblies to explore paths to a peaceful world. One year, I played Martin Luther King Junior's "I Have a Dream" speech to my class and then asked students to use "I have a dream" as their opening and write down their own dreams for the world. My sense that children and teenagers want to be seen as persons with visions of their own and respected for their ideas was affirmed and their serious and often profound thoughts were very moving.*
>
> *One by one, my students read their thoughts at a Remembrance Day assembly. Parents and other teachers said they were inspired to support children in some ways that would give them opportunities to work towards one of their dreams. One teacher said to me, "I feel like I really need to think more deeply about what I can do in the classroom and what my dreams are for my students."*

Gary Hunter (2014) suggests that we should be educating students to think about what life expects from them instead of what they can expect from life. The teacher's story above demonstrates how enriching this can be both for students and for the adults in their life. When we support our students to think about the gifts they have to offer the world, our own sense of purpose is strengthened.

One way to explore how the larger purposes you hold affect your teaching is to consider the legacy you would like to leave in relation to the children who have passed through your hands. What of most value that you teach, either directly or through your way of being, would you like to remain with students at the end of the teaching year, or five years from now, or even throughout their life? Thinking in terms of legacy always inspires us to leap toward the larger purposes of teaching and working with children. What do you hope to leave as your legacy?

Some Questions to Ask Are:

- What values have led me to become a teacher and shaped my purpose?
- What is my most noble purpose for teaching and the one most congruent with my values?
- What do I want to change about my teaching to better achieve the good I intend to do?
- Do I understand that there are many factors playing a role in my students' successes and failures and that, while I can't change many aspects of their

context, I can have a profound impact through my caring about them as persons?
- How does remembering our purpose strengthen our teaching?

Some Practices to Consider Are:

- Use your daily planner to incorporate a reminder of your larger purposes for teaching such as "value each student," "teach about fairness and justice," or "strengthen students' bonds with nature." With these reminders, you may teach to your higher values more consistently.
- Include conversations about purpose and meaning into your lessons – supporting students to reflect on what they care about and desire to do with their lives.
- Dialogue groups: Sometimes when it fits with a conversation you are having with colleagues, share what you care about and want to achieve through your teaching. Encourage others to talk about how their work gives their life meaning and purpose.

Thoughts to Remember

The purposes you intend to fulfill through your teaching should come from a deep sense of who you are as a person (i.e., they should stem from your unique combination of gifts, beliefs, and values). This means seeing your teaching as a calling to contribute in some way to making the world a better place and understanding what it is that you were called to do.

Reflecting on your reasons for becoming a teacher, reminding yourself of the good you intended to do, and acting on those intentions brings greater meaning and joy to your teaching life and protects you from burnout.

NOTES

1. Research confirms this. See, for example, Achor (2010) and Larrivee (2012).
2. A Sharing Circle is a process for respectful listening and sharing ideas and feelings. See Finney (2013), pp. 27–29, for a fuller description of ways to incorporate a Sharing Circle and its many benefits.

Chapter 4

Being Present

> When we pay attention without preconception, we are not bored or burdened by a sense that life is monotonous. Instead, our awareness of the moment is vital and invigorating. As a child, I often wondered why adults looked so bored. I didn't understand why they didn't get excited by beetles with glistening black coats of armor.... When we are not lost in our usual reactions from the past and are fully present without preference, we are able to see what a wonder and a mystery each life is. (Coleman, 2006, pp. 26–27)

Young children are attentive to their surroundings and are wonderfully surprised (and sometimes immediately frightened) by new sights, sounds, tastes, smells, and tactile experiences. Their concentration is intense and their minds don't wander as they taste dirt for the first time or bury their nose in the soft hair of the family dog. These sensual experiences can raise a range of feelings within children – some of which may be familiar and others that may be new. Even so, children remain undaunted and transfixed by their daily discoveries as they continue to explore after any initial fears have subsided.

The focus of this chapter is to bring back or heighten our abilities to be present in our daily life as adults, and to practice letting go of our thinking mind so that our attention is more tightly riveted to each and every experience. The more present we are, the more awareness we can also bring to our perceptions, understandings, and feelings. We become immersed in the actual event and are present in every sense of the word. How can we draw on our memory of childhood and learn to be more fully present in our everyday life?

While our mind contains a constant flow of thoughts that can quickly distract us from our intention to remain present to the moment in body, mind, and spirit, it is helpful to notice the particular thought we are having, let it move through our mind, and then attempt to bring our attention back to the present moment. Some people find it helpful to verbalize internally or out loud, "I am thinking of the grocery list" as a strategy to help let go of the thought before bringing themselves back to the present moment in the gym, car, or school playground.

Being present allows us to let go of the notion that we need to control or over-think every situation and, instead, it supports us in fully experiencing and, perhaps, intervening at a critical moment. In this way, we see the world more deeply, are able to participate more thoughtfully, and come to know ourselves and others at a new level.

> *It was another busy day in my multi-grade classroom. I could sense that Tom was revving himself up into a full-blown tantrum where it would be difficult for the other students to focus on their group work. I thought about his previous behaviour in groups and how other students found him difficult to work with. I managed to snap out of my reverie in time to really notice what was happening with Tom in his group. I became aware of how his attempts to contribute were being sidelined.*
>
> *This was the first time I had noticed this and was able to intervene and ask the group if each member had had an opportunity to contribute to the brainstormed list being generated. In reflecting on my day with a colleague, I acknowledged that by bringing myself back to the present moment, I had noticed a key aspect that would now help me support Tom in future group work situations.*

While being present heightens our ability to listen and pay attention to our intuition, it also allows us to notice that small miracles and surprises are a regular occurrence – from a grade 1 student exclaiming with wonder, "I can read!" to a grade 11 student pondering how their chemistry experiment blew off only their eyebrows! Our appreciation for our teaching life increases with each miracle that we witness. On some teaching days, we may even think that it is a miracle to have survived!

In everyday life, we meet individuals who seem to be comfortable with themselves in the universe. They have an authentic presence that emanates from their inner being. This authenticity does not shift as they engage with different people or different situations. While different people and situations may require us to offer different types of supports or response, when we act from an authentic center and are truly present, our actions are guided by the person we know ourselves to be.

When we are comfortable with ourselves in the world, we do not have a need to manipulate others with false praise or to pretend to be someone we are not. Authenticity means that we have a sense of who we are and have no need to repress any part of ourselves. By being ourselves, we are able to dedicate our energy to being present rather than using some of our energy to play a role or hide who we truly are.

When interacting with authentic individuals, we find them to be really "here." They are present in the moment and attentively focus on what is occurring right then. They bring a contemplative attention to their experience, sharpening their senses to interpret events in the present moment. These individuals are described as mindful and they are intensely aware of themselves and others in the environment. Each of their interactions clearly demonstrates that they are paying attention in a thoughtful, caring, and authentic way.

When we are authentic, we are able to be present without resistance (Stone Zander & Zander, 2000). We can let life unfold around us and accept the possibilities that arise. We don't have a need for events to unfold in a particular way. Instead, we are willing to surrender ourselves to the experience and participate in it with our full attention.

Authentic individuals exude a quality of receptivity, openness, and sensitivity to their sensory experiences. They know that when they are present, there is mystery and awakening, discovery and remembering, pain and suffering, along with joy and bliss. Authenticity and being present allow us to enjoy a rich contact with the world. Null (2008) explains presence as the ability to

> enjoy something that touches us and something that resonates with our essential self.... And, let it go. It stays with you in the energy you shared and the memory of that energy. That will be with you for eternity, but if you stay focused on trying to recapture it, you close yourself off to another unique and precious moment. You must be prepared for the next moment, and to be prepared for it, you must surrender the moment you're in so you're not living in the past. You're present. Being present allows you to have another blissful moment or another painful moment, but at least you are in the moment. That too will pass. Let it go. Moments must be permitted to die in order to yield to fresh new moments. In time, if you do this, your life will be filled with renewable joy. (p. 92)

Being present allows us to experience the present moment to the fullest extent possible. This includes being aware of our thoughts, feelings, and reactions. Noticing the thoughts moving through our mind, and letting them move freely through us, can help bring our attention back to the present moment. Noticing our feelings and reactions also holds us in the present moment and adds another dimension to the experience. Bringing this awareness to bear on each experience and surrendering to the thoughts, feelings, and emotions that arise allow us to come closer to living an authentic life.

Sometimes we interfere with our own authenticity because we make rules for ourselves that we are not aware of. While rules, whether imposed internally or externally, are often in place to guide or protect us, it is instructive to examine if these rules are restricting our experience or the experience of others. If so, can we find alternative ways to protect ourselves and our students so that we can allow ourselves to be present and truly soak up an experience? By being present and luxuriating in the moment, we experience the world opening up to us through the quality of attention and strong energy that we bring to the experience.

Being present allows our teaching to emanate from our authentic centre. This authenticity lets us draw on what we know to be good and true in order to guide the learning of our students with ease. When teaching authentically, we understand the importance of fully experiencing each moment and clearly see our students as individuals who deserve our utmost attention, diligence, and care.

Some Questions to Ask Are:

- When do I tend to live mostly in my thoughts? How can I integrate my thoughts with my body, feelings, senses, and heart to feel more whole and alive?
- Where in my life do I withdraw or become judgmental?
- What rules have I made for myself that limit my ability to be present?
- What do I need to let go of and what do I need to embrace, in order to be present to my students and their learning?
- How can we support each other in being our complete, whole, authentic selves?

Some Practices to Consider Are:

- Take mini-breaks to increase your sensitivity and calm the mind. For example, on the way to the staff room for lunch, step outdoors and rest your eyes on nature at a distance while you take three deep breaths.
- Focus on the full experience of being with your students. Listen to them with openness and genuine interest. Really look at your students and notice their quiet joy, surprise, or, perhaps, their discouragement as they engage with different materials and questions.
- Dialogue groups: Make "Being Present – Being Ourselves" a focus for a collegial gathering. Discuss how we can support each other to be comfortable with ourselves as we are and reduce the stresses and judgments that take us away from being present to our school life as it unfolds.

Thoughts to Remember

People who are able to be present to all that life is and that life offers have an authentic presence and seem comfortable with themselves in a way that draws others to them. We can increase our presence by activating all of our senses and tuning into our body and breathing. We can also increase our presence by being open to what the moment brings and by allowing ourselves to surrender and experience the moment to the fullest.

The ability to be fully present in as many moments as we can brings us wonderful gifts including the joy of being alive, that of feeling completely awake and receptive to all that a moment contains, including our place in the energy flow of the classroom. It also helps us to be aware of our students and to accept the ups and downs of classroom life, knowing that no situation is permanent, and with this acceptance comes the knowledge that we can affect the moment and contribute to a richer learning experience for ourselves and for our students.

Chapter 5

Honoring Our Suffering

> Give sorrow words. The grief that does not speak
> Knits up the o'er wrought heart and bids it break.
>
> —William Shakespeare, *Macbeth*

One of the most important actions we can adopt as teachers is to feel our feelings, to take the time to feel our pain, our compassion, and our joy. Most spiritual traditions include practices for accepting and understanding our own suffering – the ways we have been hurt. This is the work of a lifetime. This is the work we most often avoid. Too many unrecognized or unacknowledged hurts from the past build walls around the heart. In order to protect ourselves, we become distant from our own feelings. A sad effect of this distancing is that it makes it hard to recognize and feel the suffering of our students and others we care about.

> Telling your unhappy stories, calling up memories you might rather leave untouched, and remembering people who didn't help you much on your way is all valuable – your bad experiences are as much a part of you as the good ones, and to be fully present to your current work, you have to include them as well. (Moore, 2008, p. 47)

Pain and suffering are very much a part of being human – they cannot be avoided and there is much to learn from them. It does take courage to face the pain we carry, and try to understand it and the ways it may still be influencing our behavior and thinking patterns. As part of this way of honoring our pain, it is important to understand that our past is not our fate. It is an important part of who we are and our memories of the forces that have shaped us will contain both blessings and troubles.

In his book *The Wise Heart*, Kornfield (2008) offers some advice about the process of facing and then letting go of the causes of our suffering. He suggests that it means not trying to get rid of these experiences but rather softening into a state of allowing them to be part of us, perhaps by saying, "This happened to me." He says, "The softening brings a felt sense of release in the body and mind" (p. 248).

Rohr (2011) also sees understanding suffering as a spiritual practice which can reveal how we remain a constant problem to ourselves, and help open up "new spaces within us for learning and loving" (p. 68). Creating a narrative to describe the times when we have been frightened or misunderstood, or when we have suffered or caused suffering is one method that can help us explore the causes of emotional pain and its effects, and integrate past and present suffering into our life in an empathetic way.

Seigel and Hartzell (2003) describe new findings in neuro-social psychology[1] which contribute to understanding the roles of the emotions in our personal lives. They explain that self-reflection and understanding our internal processes allow us to develop a greater range of responses to the behaviors of others. Awareness opens up the possibilities of *choosing* our responses rather than being controlled by emotional reactions created more by our past experiences than the present situation. Appendices A and B describe other ways to develop greater emotional strength.

In reflecting on our own suffering, it may be helpful to distinguish between the different causes of emotional pain. There is the pain we cause ourselves through actions we regret or through dwelling on past failures. We are sometimes better at recognizing transgressions against us than we are at acknowledging those of our own. It takes courage to do this form of soul-searching, but looking in the mirror at our own shortcomings can be a way to come to terms with our humanity and that of others. It can relieve us of a burden of guilt and increase our capacity for compassionate understanding.

Another form of emotional pain comes from the unkindness, rejection, or unfairness of others. Even when we know we did not deserve ill treatment, we feel the pain of it. When we see deeply into this pain, we are faced again with the human condition – when someone suffers from hurtful treatment and unmet needs, they sometimes pass this suffering along. Children, teenagers, and adults who have been emotionally hurt often find subtle and not so subtle ways to hurt others.

Yet another cause of emotional pain that is not always recognized is that of not being really *seen*, appreciated, and accepted for who we are – particularly who we are on the inside. Such experiences can cause us to reject parts of ourselves and spend large parts of our lives in trying to please others and be the person they want rather than being our authentic self. Prolonged fear is also a form of suffering.

When I was in grade two, I was very afraid of my teacher – much too afraid to ask or answer a question. I was afraid to request that I be excused to go to the bathroom and the inevitable happened. I sat for the rest of the morning with wet pants and a telltale puddle under my desk. When I think of that experience I can still relive the shame I felt. I remained afraid of that teacher the whole year.

It was a very hard year despite the fact that I was a good student. The only redeeming thing about my experiences that year is that they stayed in my memory and helped me to never deny access to the bathroom to any students in my own teaching career. I realized there are very simple ways to avoid this permission being abused and much to be gained from trusting my students.

Perhaps the deepest kind of suffering we experience is from the death, loss, or suffering of those we love. The grief that results is not easily avoided and often calls to be shared. Seeking spiritual supports is another way that humans use to keep their hearts open in the face of devastating pain. An important part of this willingness to explore our suffering is that it can lead us into an understanding of and real concern for others – those within our circle of daily experiences, those we pass on the street, and all those human lives that reach us through news media, literature, or biography. The circle can ever widen to encompass the earth and all living beings. This is a journey without end – one in which the heart is becoming a vessel of wisdom and love.

Looking back on our past, we may be able to recognize those moments and experiences when our childhood was not always happy. We may also recognize that we still feel anger at the person or persons who treated us badly and that we are carrying this anger in our body. Kindness is often a large part of our nature as teachers making it harder to recognize that we feel anger at times. Seeing through any anger we carry and acknowledging it without passing it on can make us more authentic.

Students are quick to recognize when their teachers are not fully genuine; they have greater trust and respect for those who are. The attempt to uncover pain from our past and to understand how it may be affecting our present is worthwhile in that it offers us another context for developing self-understanding, increasing compassion, extending forgiveness, and for dismantling any walls we have created to protect our heart from further emotional pain. The soul work of facing the suffering we carry, rather than breaking us, can make us stronger, more compassionate, and better able to recognize the suffering of others, including our students.

We gain strength by recognizing the suffering in our lives and allowing the feelings that result to become a form of self-compassion. The following Chinese proverb provides a striking reminder of the difference between facing our suffering and prolonged dwelling in it:

You cannot prevent the birds of sorrow from flying over your head, but you can prevent them from building nests in your hair.

Some Questions to Ask Are:

- What fears and anxieties have caused me suffering? What kinds of things hurt me the most? Am I aware of the patterns within my emotional pain? Have any of my hurts and sorrows become buried in my body as anger?
- Am I able to feel the emotions of others close to me? How can I experience their pain without distancing myself from it or, alternatively, without being swallowed up by it?
- What supports or practices can help me to face my suffering?
- How do we recognize when one of our students is suffering? Can we distinguish between the hurtful behaviors of a student and the unmet needs and painful feelings that may be causing the student to harm others?

Some Practices to Consider Are:

- Recall a time in your life when you experienced emotional pain. Ask yourself questions such as, "What were the causes of my suffering at that time? Within that experience, did I feel understood and supported by anyone? Can I feel gratitude for any support I received and face and accept any emotional pain I felt?" Sit quietly and breathe softly for a few minutes. Close the experience by affirming that suffering is a part of human life.
- Tune into your body and see if you can tell where you are holding sorrows from a time in your past when you suffered. Offer yourself as much love and compassion as you can for the hurts and fears of that time. Tighten your hands into fists. Hold the tension, and then release it, allowing the hands to be soft. Work with this as a metaphor for how suffering, past pain, angers, and regrets feel in the body and how calm we feel when we let them go.
- Dialogue groups: Reflect together on the many causes of emotional suffering that students may experience at home, with peers, or in the classroom and how this is reflected in their behavior. Raise ideas of how as teachers we can recognize a student who is suffering and respond to it without violating their privacy. You might also explore the idea that the more we can feel our own suffering and have compassion for ourselves, the more we can increase our awareness of the emotional pain of our students.

Thoughts to Remember

Psychologists, spiritual leaders, and others who have faced their pain and sorrow understand what an important life task it is to reflect on, accept, and soften to our suffering. We honor our pain because it is a powerful teacher and because it is a part of the human condition. As humans, we are vulnerable to suffering and we are capable of nobility of soul, of being courageous and compassionate.

We can learn to face and use our suffering to gain emotional and spiritual strength and grow in compassion, kindness, and greater understanding of the suffering of others. Our courage in the face of sorrow also brings the gift of greater flexibility and creativeness in responding to others and daily events. Attending to our pain, we become stronger and more tender-hearted.

NOTE

1. An integrated human science that brings together findings from research into the workings of the human brain, social influences on the mind and emotions, and patterns of human behavior and the meanings they hold for individuals.

Chapter 6

Trusting Our Inner Knowledge

> BEN: Listen. Can you hear that? It falls across you like a blanket,
> Like a benediction, if you listen, if you
> Learn to listen.
> There it is again; hear it?
> Silence.
> In that silence lies more truth than in any words.
> In language as we use it, there's not much truth. There's truth here
> (Indicates the chest.) and here (Indicates the stomach). Other
> places. On the face perhaps. But on the tongue?
>
> (Excerpt from "Atlantis," a play by Maureen Hunter, 1997,
> Winnipeg MB: SciroccoDrama/J. Gordon Shillingford
> Publishing Inc., p. 13. Reproduced with permission.)

How many times have we ignored that little voice within us only to discover later that we should have paid attention to our initial internal response to a situation? It is important to emphasize here that an initial internal response is not necessarily an impulsive response. There is a wide gap between an inner integrated intuitive response and an outer fractured impulsive response. Hoff (1982) suggests that our inner knowledge can be relied on and that it can guide us regarding the best course of action.

Ferguson (1980) sees intuition as encompassing intellect and describes it as transcendent reasoning. She believes that our intuition represents "the brain's capacity for simultaneous analysis we cannot consciously track and comprehend" (p. 107). Neuroscience has shown that her insight into how intuition works is true and a gift we rely on extensively without knowing *how* we know how to do much of what we do.

Intuition brings together our mind, spirit, emotions, and physical bodies to provide a type of "embodied knowing" (Orr, 1992). This knowing supports us in recognizing and trusting our inner knowledge, and in paying attention to the voice within us. Relying on our inner voice allows us to access wisdom that is already there. This reliance requires an element of trust. We need to trust that the inner messages our body is giving us are reliable. We need to trust that students can learn and that learning will happen with our practiced and intuitive guidance and support. The more we are open to this guidance, the more we can receive.

Part of trusting our inner knowledge is having a sense of what is true, what is in harmony, and what is beneficial for our well-being. Rather than narrowing our attention into our head and the thinking that goes on there, can we widen our attention to also feel into our heart, into our emotions, into our gut? Can we move from the circuitous thinking of the brain to the comfort and knowing of the heart? The mind analyses, while the heart synthesizes. The heart sees the world in a different way. Peaceful energetic shifts take place inside us when we *know* with our heart.

Sylvia Ashton-Warner, the gifted teacher of young Maori children, trusted her insights and deep knowing to find ways to teach that were in harmony with her intuitive understanding of children. She saw and felt the needs of her students through this intuitive lens and wrote, "Children have two visions, the inner and the outer. Of the two, the inner vision is brighter" (1963, p. 29). We want our young people to retain this inner vision or intuitive sense of their world because it is a gift that they can trust – developing as it does from keen observation and emotional acuity. A wonderful use of our intuition as teachers is to see and support the intuitions and vision of our students.

Intuition is like an inner gaze that is not bound by linear time. When we adopt an inner gaze, we step into our vast free nature. We relax into eternal time and are able to access knowledge that comes from the heart and is echoed in the stomach. Our hearts have their own way of seeing things. When we pay attention with our hearts, our inner knowledge is freed up and bubbles to the surface of our consciousness. Perhaps, as the character Ben suggests in the opening quote, we would be wise to let our attention drop down to the areas below our head – to our heart and our stomach – in order to find the truth.

Intuition has long been a fascination of humans; but until the 1990s, researchers couldn't study brain impulses and connections related to intuition directly. Since that time, neuroscience and psychological research have produced a great deal of understanding of "eureka" or "aha" moments, intuitions, insights, and what are often called gut feelings. Their findings are particularly relevant for teachers who, due to the fast pace of classroom life, need to think on their feet and rely on mental processing that happens so rapidly that it is best described as intuitive knowledge or instinct.

Scientists[1] have described intuition as rapid cognition, knowing something without knowing how you know it, and as a process that allows us to know something directly without analysis, thus bridging the gap between conscious and unconscious thoughts. An intuition is considered to be the result of the way our brains store, process, and retrieve information on a subconscious level. The brain draws on past experiences and external cues to make a quick decision possible without conscious analysis.

There is a degree of unpredictability that goes with life in the classroom, and the more interactive and student-centered a teacher's practice is, the more likely and often that their intuition will be used. It is helpful then to be aware of how reliable our intuitive processes are. Research findings from the fields of psychology, neuroscience, and education describe factors that make "aha" moments, insights, and intuitions more trustworthy and those that hinder their reliability. They also describe ways to strengthen our intuitive abilities.

Three factors are important in relation to knowing whether you can trust your rapid responses and decisions when having to think on your feet in the classroom. One is the amount of experience you have with different instructional approaches and the extent of your knowledge of effective responses to student behaviors. Another way to describe this is to say the more schema or mental models you have to draw upon in relation to the subject matter, best teaching practices, and the needs and behavior patterns of your students, the more likely that your intuitions will be trustworthy.

A second factor that makes your rapid insights reliable is the extent to which you are aware of your own biases that may cause you to respond better to some students and some ideas more than others. You can improve the reliability of your intuitions also by reflecting back on how well your on-the-spot decisions have worked in the past. Our effectiveness will continue to improve when we "reflect in action" and later reflect *on* the actions we took.

Other findings suggest that "gut instincts" or the feelings that come from the body are usually trustworthy. They may not tell you exactly how to respond but they do alert you to situations where something is not quite right. This ability to sense what is happening and how you feel about it is strengthened when you pay attention to your heartbeat as well. The heart or feeling centre of our being, sometimes also referred to as our soul, is another source of intuitions or a way to do a double check on our first impulses.

> *I was pretty pleased with the classroom set-up that I had designed using learning stations where students would rotate through the various stations in 20-minute intervals. On the third morning, my stomach started to feel uneasy. I ignored it as I felt it was merely a sign of tiredness on my part. That evening, I was walking our dog and I reflected on my uneasiness. It was coming from somewhere, but where? I realized that I was uncomfortable with the lack of choice that I was*

providing for my students with regard to the amount of time that they could spend at each station. I solved this by giving students a block of time to work through four stations where they could choose the amount of time per station.

We can strengthen our abilities for insight and intuition in a number of ways including taking time for solitude, slowing down, and letting our dreams and feelings, and the images and sounds in our environment take us out of our analytic thinking mode to a state of softer, wider thoughts and images. When we have been ruminating on a classroom problem for a long time, it is often effective to stop this analytic thinking and the anxiousness it creates. As the teacher reflecting on the timing of her learning stations found, it is sometimes helpful to change our setting and our activity to a simple or physical task – putting our problem on the back burner. Research suggests that in situations like this, solutions are likely to just pop into our mind while we are doing a mundane task like peeling potatoes.

Meditation and yoga are also good ways to slow down analytic thought, anxieties, worries, and mental list-making, and to become more mindful of our body and the environment around us. Research has not confirmed that paying greater attention to our dreams improves our intuitive abilities and their accuracy directly, but they do widen the lens of our attention and offer more possibilities than those seen by analytic thinking alone. As well, paying attention to coincidences and surprising connections and how often they occur is a way to stay aware of more of daily life and the possible meanings it contains. Noticing these coincidences is another indirect way to strengthen our intuitive abilities.

Trusting our inner knowledge requires courage – one that comes from an integrated mind, body, heart, and spirit ethos. This integration is accomplished through mindfulness, gratefulness, and other opening energy practices that connect us to ourselves, to others, and to mother earth and the wider environment. These practices and energies open us up and allow us to experience our whole selves. When we are whole, it is easier to pay attention to our intuitive knowledge for we are then at peace and realize our "oneness" with the universe. This peace provides a warm, nurturing environment that supports us and our students as we learn about the world and each other together. Trusting our intuition and that of our students may provide new openings for learning.

Some Questions to Ask Are:

- In what situations have I trusted my inner guidance – in my personal life or in my teaching life?
- How does listening to my heart contribute to my sense of harmony and well-being? In what ways does this affect my personal and professional life?

- In what ways does a particular decision or behavior, based on my intuition, feel "right" to me? How can I use these "ways" to guide me?
- What serendipitous moments did I notice in the last week/month? What meanings did they convey to me?
- Are there strategies we can use to drop down from our head to our heart to find our inner knowledge? How can we incorporate these strategies into our school life?

Some Practices to Consider Are:

- In your daily life, pay attention to "gut" or initial reactions to situations and consider if such reactions are, perhaps, messages from your heart or inner guide upon which to act. Practice listening and responding from the heart.
- When deciding on a course of action in your teaching or your personal life, consider how true or harmonious the action seems with who you are and what you value.
- Dialogue groups: Make teacher intuition a focus for one of your times together asking, "To what extent does each of us use it in our teaching, how does it benefit our students, and how aware are we of these classroom actions that are guided by intuition?" Reflect on how intuitive actions may differ from impulsive ones.

Thoughts to Remember

Inner knowledge, often called intuition, is an aspect of our intellect – one that integrates head knowledge with the knowledge that comes from our body and heart. The stomach or gut often sends us a message about what is happening and how we feel about it. Such knowledge is trustworthy and a way to check on first impulses. Part of trusting our intuition is having a sense of what is true, what is in harmony, and what is beneficial for our well-being.

Inner knowledge is a gift that benefits us and our students. Relying on our inner voice allows us to access wisdom that is already there and can put us in touch with a larger, holistic view and the voice of the universe. The more we draw on this knowledge, the more guidance we receive.

NOTE

1. The ideas drawn upon in this chapter include a wealth of information from research in the fields of psychology, neuroscience, and education including those of Hogarth (2001), Meyers (2002), Burke and Sadler-Smith (2006), and Kounios and Beeman (2015).

Chapter 7

Practicing Self-compassion

> We now see that the only way that we could love ourselves is by loving others, and the only way that we could truly love others is to love ourselves. The difference between self-love and love of others is very small, once we really understand. Taking this truth into our hearts and actions is truly life changing. (Fischer, 2012, p. 13)

Love is our true nature. We may forget this at times when we are experiencing feelings of regret. At such times, our task is to trust our own inner goodness and remember that nothing in life and no action of ours can permanently destroy our goodness. The instinct to teach comes from this center of kindness which can't be truly lost, but we can forget or doubt it when it is shaken by some troubling experience.

If you are reading this book, it is already clear that you care a lot about your students and the quality of their experiences with you. An important step in doing no harm is to not harm our self with critical and negative thoughts about some lapse or failure that shakes our belief in our own worthiness and goodness. For some reason, we believe if we criticize ourselves, it will lead to improvements. Or, if we are harsh with ourselves, we will become kinder. This has never been true. Only love leads to love.

Our ability to be sensitive to the feelings of others depends on this ability to understand our own feelings and have compassion for ourselves. Eleanor Roosevelt said this simply and powerfully when she commented that friendship with one's self is all important, because without it, one cannot be friends with anyone else in the world. When your kind heart fails you momentarily in a classroom interaction, it is important to act to restore the good relationship that you desire with your students. It is equally important to restore your compassionate relationship with yourself.

It is helpful in most areas of inner growth and strengthening of the spirit, to start from a modest and manageable place. In terms of self-compassion, some basics include the idea that feelings of kindness for ourselves begin with the obvious but important recognition that we are alive and that with life comes vulnerability. Like all creatures, we have bodies that can cause us pain. Like all humans, we have minds that can think hurtful thoughts as well as healing thoughts. Our thoughts can be misguided or inspiring. In both cases, it is good to remember that they are just thoughts, not reality.

On the other hand, thoughts can be powerful, so it's better to have kind ones toward ourselves. It is possible to be honest with our self without being overly critical. (See Appendix B for ideas that support this practice.) The motivation to be kind is helped by the recognition that this can only stem from feelings of kindness toward the self. The recognition that with life comes vulnerability can be the motivation to treat ourselves with kindness. The simple act of wishing ourselves well, through repeating good wishes for our well-being often in a day and every day creates greater happiness. "May I be happy today. May I be kind to myself."

Research shows that practicing self-compassion contributes to beneficial changes such as:

- Modulating hormonal functioning, especially of oxytocin and cortisol
- Moderating depression and anxiety
- Increasing emotional well-being
- Mitigating negative thinking, including rumination. (Cottler, 2014)

In Cottler's view, "Being compassionate with yourself generates acceptance of your humanness and the humanness of others, an essential quality for a fuller awakening" (2014). This idea of recognizing our common humanity is also helpful in developing greater humility – a sense of our ordinariness that keeps our pride in check. When we feel we need to do and be better than others, it is hard to accept experiences where we fail or someone else seems to achieve more than we do. With self-compassion, we let go of competition. We act in ways that we believe are kind, just, and well thought out. We do our best and can happily appreciate the accomplishments of others.

Compassion involves a kind of deep listening and seeing. It often requires gentleness and stillness.[1] Within such stillness, we begin to understand that compassion emanates from an open heart. Another way to understand the gentle quality of self-compassion is the idea that compassion does not force us to be different but allows us to be who we are. When we can accept our inner life as spacious and are able to contain all our thoughts and feelings, we let go of a lot of the tension that wears us down. Practicing self-compassion on a daily basis "generates, solidifies, and strengthens deeply positive experiences in your life that literally etch into the brain" (Cottler, 2014).

For Neff (2013), self-compassion is the key to happiness and to resilience. She finds self-compassion to be a robust predictor of wellness. Whereas self-esteem deserts you when you fail, self-compassion remains whether you are successful or not. Neff outlines three important practices related to self-compassion:

1. Treat yourself with care and kindness
2. Recognize your imperfections as part of a shared human experience
3. Stay with your experience in a nonjudgmental way – see things as they are, no more and no less.

Neff sees the driving force of self-compassion as the desire to thrive and be happy, and to alleviate suffering. She recommends that we relate kindly to ourselves and treat ourselves as human beings worthy of care and respect.

Dr. Sylvia Boorstein (2007), a psychologist and meditation teacher, describes one way that she practices having a kinder and gentler response when she is experiencing emotional pain. She talks to herself using language that strengthens her self-compassion. She gives the following example. "[Sylvia], you are in pain. Relax. Take a breath. Let's pay attention to what is happening. Then we'll figure out what to do" (p. 10).

> *I have noticed that I still carry regrets for actions of mine that didn't turn out well long after they happened. Years later, something will trigger a memory of a response to a student that was hurtful and I feel the remorse all over again. It is very hard to accept that teaching is not something that can be perfected. The nature of human relationships and the pace of classroom life work against this. I am trying to remember this – one way I have of being kinder to myself, is to say, "You did the best you could at the time. You do learn from your mistakes. Now it's time to let it go."*

Teaching involves countless opportunities to act sensitively, to see our own goodness, and to forgive our lapses. If you are like most humans, you often focus on the times when you feel you have violated your moral code and forget to notice and remember all the ways in which you have helped students and others each day. Perhaps, you are setting standards for yourself that are too high to be consistently achieved.

These standards may permeate your life in terms of your teaching practice, your responsibilities at home, and even your recreational pursuits, leaving little time in your inner life to relax and just be. It would be beneficial – an act of kindness – if you could relax your expectations for yourself in ways that allow you more opportunities to just enjoy the moment, and bring you more calmness and peace of mind. You *can* learn to turn your loving heart on to yourself in an act of kindness.

Some Questions to Ask Are:

- How do I maintain a belief in my essential goodness, the kindness of my heart?
- Am I a perfectionist? In what ways do I use perfectionism as a strategy to protect myself? How can I let go of this strategy and, instead, practice self-compassion in relation to my perceived mistakes?
- Am I able to laugh at myself?
- Do I tend to hold on to regrets for things done or left undone? Do I excessively analyse some event in my teaching that upset me, going over it again and again? How might I let it go and dwell with kind awareness in the present?
- How would our school life be different if we set the intention to be more self-compassionate each day?

Some Practices to Consider Are:

- Create a visual image of your softest, most loving self. See the gentleness and kindness in your eyes, hear the warmth in your voice. Use this visualization when you need it most, perhaps before embarking on a difficult conversation, and when you need this support in order to restore warmheartedness and feel compassion for yourself.
- Develop greater awareness of the standards you set for yourself and the ways they enrich your life or deplete your ability to be self-compassionate. For example, do you feel a need to have attractive bulletin boards that are changed frequently? Is this need more to display student work in order to support learning, or to demonstrate your competence to others? Are there many areas in your life where you are good enough and feel positive self-acceptance?
- Dialogue groups: Make self-compassion a focus of one occasion together. You might focus on the ways that the high standards we set for ourselves as teachers can be damaging to well-being, even though they may be helpful in terms of student learning. Share ideas as to which standards benefit students the most and if there are ways to support each other to make teacher well-being more central. You might work from the idea that a tired teacher or one carrying a lot of stress cannot create a very healthy learning environment or be a role model of wholeness.

Thoughts to Remember

You are a good person. At your center is a loving heart and a desire to help and heal. Nothing in life and no actions of yours can permanently destroy this essential goodness. We can face our mistakes and the actions we regret with gentleness, make amends when that is possible, and let them go softly, and show generosity toward the self we intended to be. Bringing more kindness to your self-talk on a daily basis leads to a happier life.

The gifts of having compassion for ourselves include greater acceptance, relaxation, and appreciation for the self we are right now, in this present moment, and human form. With self-compassion comes greater peace of mind and love and compassion for others.

NOTE

1. Mindfulness practices support the development of gentleness and stillness and greater self-acceptance. See Appendix A.

Chapter 8

Reflecting on Our Practice

> After wandering along the lane for two hours, giving way to every variety of thought; re-considering events, determining probabilities, and reconciling herself as well as she could, to a change so sudden and so important, fatigue, and a recollection of her long absence, made her at length return home; and she entered the house with the wish of appearing cheerful as usual, and the resolution of repressing such reflections as must make her unfit for conversation.
>
> —Jane Austen

Elizabeth Bennet's reflection, as shown in the opening quote above, concerns the unwinding of her prejudice against the apparent arrogance of her suitor, Fitzgerald Darcy. Throughout the novel, *Pride and Prejudice*, Elizabeth engages in many bouts of reflection, both privately and in discussion with others. In the excerpt above, she is reliving events and problem solving as she walks. Reflection helps Elizabeth think more deeply about how she conducts her social life through self-questioning, analyzing actions and their effects, and considering alternatives.

Reflective practice is a strong way to increase our awareness of our values, our habits, and our interactions.[1] It allows us to think on our feet as well as relive incidents after they occur. Thinking on our feet includes noticing when an adjustment to a lesson, assignment, or response is needed "on the spot," whereas reflecting after a lesson allows us to consider alternatives for future practice. Both situations help us to learn from experience. Taking a moment to reflect both during and following an activity sharpens our powers of observation and supports us in responding appropriately.

As we make multiple decisions in our day-to-day classroom life, adopting a reflective stance can soften the hard edges of a trying moment or a lesson not going well. For example, if it is evident that students are not grasping a particular concept, it is helpful to stop and consider the following: "Am I being clear? Would drawing a diagram be helpful? Can I think of an interesting simile that might support students' understanding? "

Reflection-in-action is challenging as it requires turning one's attention inward while continuing to facilitate learning outwardly. Some touchstones to support this type of reflection include asking questions internally such as: "Have I lost anybody? How am I feeling?" Questions such as these, posed internally during teaching and learning activities, will help us make changes on the spot to maximize students' learning or raise our awareness of tension in our body.

Examining our practice allows us to see if our daily words and actions reflect our personal theories and beliefs, and may even raise them to our consciousness for the first time. For example, while we believe in providing scaffolds (such as explaining a new concept with alternative examples) to support student learning, are we actually practicing it regularly in order to help students move on to the next step or level? While we may have a strong belief that all students can learn regardless of gender, race, or ability, does our daily classroom practice consistently reflect this belief?

> *I had just finished what I thought was a successful end-of-day lesson and I was talking over my lesson with a colleague. I had asked him to sit in on my lesson to provide me with feedback regarding a particular group of students who were having difficulty grasping a foundational scientific concept. After our discussion, my colleague handed me a checklist that he had created to show my interactions with the students in the class. As I looked over the checklist, I noticed that my interactions with the boys in the class exceeded my interactions with the girls by a factor of 5 to 1. Essentially, I was giving the boys in my class (regardless of ability) five times the attention that I was giving the girls.*
>
> *What did this mean? Did I think that boys needed more help than girls? Did I believe, at some level, that girls were smarter than boys and did not need my guidance or questioning? Alternatively, was I socializing the girls to be quiet and obedient? This reflection raised many questions for me and I began to look more closely at my daily interactions with my students.*

The reflection above caused this teacher to focus on the qualities of fairness and respect being enacted through her classroom practice.

Research shows that engaging in reflective practice helps us to understand our teaching life more deeply by raising our tacit knowledge and informal theories for examination. Reflecting on our practice not only deepens our self-awareness but also allows us to learn from our mistakes. We want to ensure, however, that our reflections do not become overly critical and leave us discouraged.

It is helpful to adopt a practice that focuses equally on what went well in our teaching day, noting such things as a few minutes when the students all seemed at peace and focused on their learning or a short, supportive exchange we had with a student or colleague. In this way, reflections can also strengthen our store of spiritual energy. While reflections can occur mid-teaching or during quiet moments after a lesson or unit of study, sometimes talking with others can prompt new understanding to arise.

Thurgood Sagal (2009) finds that teachers talking among themselves about their practice can play a valuable role in "supporting further thinking, new understanding, and related practice" (p. 58). That is why informal conversations in hallways, classroom doorways, staffrooms, and other venues are important and often meet professional as well as social and emotional needs. Taking time to admire and discuss colleagues' teaching and learning projects can be initiated by individual teachers and can result in new understandings for everyone involved. Reflecting with a colleague in this positive way supports further dialogue and can become a reciprocal practice. Regularly reflecting on our own or with others creates an environment where reflection is embedded in the culture and ethos of the school.

Thurgood Sagal (2009) describes critical features for supporting personal and professional reflection in schools, and argues for the valuing and normalizing of reflective practice:

> These features require a school environment where risk taking is the "norm," where teachers' knowledge is valued, where student learning drives decision making, and where the school involves the community to support the learning of all children and youth. (p. 118)

This is a vision not easily attained, but is important to work toward, and valuable for assessing the quality of reflective practice in our schools.

To support the incorporation of these key features, it is necessary that we as teachers are involved in determining potential avenues for engaging in reflective practice and, thereby, understanding our professional and personal life more deeply. While contributing to the development of school and system structures that support reflective practice is valuable, it is also important that we find *individual* ways to reflect on our achievements and challenges on a regular basis. In this way, reflective practice becomes an integral part of our teaching life.

An important and challenging focus for our reflections has to do with thinking deeply about how our identity, how the way we view ourselves, and how we have become the person we are shape our teaching. Knowing the influences on our early lives and ways in which they may have motivated us to become the particular kind of teacher we are is useful and it helps to keep our motivations for teaching clear.

Nieto (2003) describes the importance of developing autobiographical knowledge and highlights the link between self-reflection, self-knowledge, and kind, respectful teaching:

> I believe that all educators, if they are to become effective teachers of their students, need to confront tough questions about their identities and motivations; they need to think about why they do the things they do and ask if there might be a better way of reaching their students; they need to reflect on how a word, a gesture, or an action might inspire or wound for life. (p. 32)

A natural rhythm for incorporating reflective practice in schools is to reflect at the end of the school day, either alone or with a colleague. Reflection at this time of day can foster closure and provide a transition period between the school day and one's personal life. We are reflective practitioners because we care about the quality of student learning, our personal growth, and the safety and warmth of the school atmosphere, and especially because reflection is a central part of what it means to be a teacher. It is simply what teachers do.

Some Questions to Ask Are:

- Who am I? What were the influences that shaped the way I am as a teacher?
- What do I value and want to promote through my teaching? In what ways does my daily practice reflect my values and beliefs about teaching, learning, my students, and myself?
- What reflective practices strengthen my store of spiritual energy? For example, am I energized by discussing the results of a lesson with a colleague or by reflecting quietly as I walk home?
- In reviewing my reflections over time, can I see what my potential is and the limits I put on it with regard to my teaching practice?
- When might opportunities for reflection, either alone or with each other, occur? How can we increase these opportunities at our school and get administrative support?

Some Practices to Consider Are:

- Reflect upon a lesson (either alone or with a colleague), what went well, what surprised you, in what ways it reflected your values and deepest beliefs about teaching, and how this knowledge might change your practice. Notice the effect this reflection has on your spirit.
- Find a moment at the beginning or end of your teaching day to enjoy the quiet stillness of your classroom to reflect upon how you have created a physical space that supports your spirit and is conducive to teaching and

learning. Turn your reflections to the social, cultural, and emotional space of your classroom and how you might make adjustments to this sacred ecological space so that you and your students have room to breathe life into the curriculum.
- Dialogue groups: Use journals as a tool for self-exploration and to support conversations with colleagues. Respond to some of the *Questions to Ask* as starters for your writing and dialogue.

Thoughts to Remember

Refection is a state of mind that is most helpful when it involves a soft, free exploration rather than one of rumination, perseveration, and worry. We learn most when we feel open and confident in the intentions we have for our practice. When our commitment is to supporting student growth in a holistic manner that attends to their hearts and bodies as well as their minds, our reflections will be broader and encompass more of our practice. In this way, we are more likely to see avenues for future practice and connections between the physical, social, and emotional environment and the lessons we teach.

It is important to remember that reflection may reveal roadblocks to learning; but it isn't about self-condemnation so much as about seeing what you are doing, and exploring avenues for change. Keeping your reflective practice open and avoiding being overly self-critical may reap new insights and inspirations that ensure more student learning and a deeper understanding of your pedagogical practice.

NOTE

1. This belief is supported by the work of Donald Schön (1983) and grounded in the research of Thurgood Sagal (2009).

Part II

TO IMBUE OUR CHALLENGES WITH HEART

"Doing it right" can be an obstacle to caring. When we are totally focused on "covering the material," preoccupied with competence and success, we often forget to open our hearts to our students. . . . Our hearts can also become blocked when we are attached to a particular plan, technique, or approach in the classroom. If we keep our hearts open, we can see the unique needs of our students and discover entirely different ways to reach our larger goals.[1]

NOTE

1. Kessler, R. (2001). "Soul of Students, Soul of Teachers" in Lantieri (2001), p. 123.

Chapter 9

Preserving Our Integrity

> Wholeness, a psychological state of internal harmony and consistent moral character, best captures the essence of integrity. (Killinger, 2007, p. 12)

Teaching contexts, like all others that involve human relationships, do raise moral dilemmas that test us. In meeting these dilemmas well, Palmer (1998) sees wholeness as central. This is evident in his claim that "good teaching cannot be reduced to technique; good teaching comes from the identity and integrity of the teacher" (p. 10).

A person with integrity is trustworthy in words and deeds, yet flexible in meeting the needs of the moment. What is consistent are the values they hold and moral standards they do their best to adhere to within changing contexts. Sometimes there are gray areas where two values or moral standards conflict, thus integrity also demands that we spend time in reflection and turning to others for their thoughts. These are challenges that each of us struggles with in maintaining a whole and authentic self in difficult situations.

For Rosenberg (2003), integrity is a basic need that we all have. He defines integrity as including authenticity, creativity, meaning, and self-worth (p. 54). By being ourselves, drawing on our creativity, finding meaning, and acknowledging our self-worth, we embrace a more whole view of ourselves – a view that contributes to fulfilling our basic need for integrity. In Rohr's (2011) complementary view, "Integrity largely has to do with purifying our intentions and a growing honesty about our actual motives. It is hard work. Most often we don't pay attention to that inner task until we have had some kind of fall or failure in our outer tasks" (p. xv).

Thinking about our intentions and why we want to do something may reveal aspects of ourselves that we do not want to see. It may also reveal something that helps us understand an underlying need that we have. This understanding will help us see ourselves more clearly. Such clarity is a strong base from which to face the moral challenges that life in schools offers us. For example, is it possible to maintain our integrity when school policy conflicts with our professional beliefs and values? What happens when we are not comfortable listening to gossip or negative comments made regarding a child or their parents? Many teachers experience such conflict as threats to their character, conscience, and self-respect, making it difficult to maintain their integrity.[1]

Palmer (2001) agrees and suggests that we can "no longer collaborate in something that violates [our] own integrity" (p. 5). In order to find professional fulfillment, we need to see an alignment between our ethical convictions and our daily actions. When a policy or school decision makes this difficult, we feel this disconnect deeply and look for ways to seek support and take action in order to maintain our integrity. Often the only possible solution is to speak up and name what we feel is not in the interest of students or our professionalism, and find ways to minimize potential damage to our students and ourselves.

Our integrity can be relentless. It calls on us to face things even when we are afraid. Kelm (2008) suggests that:

> The secret is in learning to turn the pain and fear of the negative emotion into hope and inspiration for change. It's learning to see the improvement that is needed, but rather than *moving away* from pain or fear, you *move toward* what you want [original emphasis]. (p. 135)

By focusing on the intended results, our energy and efforts become directed in positive ways that align our actions with our convictions.

For many of us, acting on our convictions and standing up for our beliefs is a way of life. For others, our personality may prevent us from speaking up even though we may desire to do so. Lantieri (2001) stresses the importance of being "field independent . . . possessing the capacity to stand against the crowd or work against convention" (p. 19). Are there particular virtues that we can draw upon to support ourselves in doing this? Honesty is one. Our love for our profession and our students' well-being comes to mind. Also our commitment to eliminate prejudice, racism, and other biased views that damage some individuals and groups is fundamental. A capacity to stand against the crowd is related to Rosenberg's authenticity and Rohr's purification of intentions. If we are clear on our motivation and beliefs, this provides us with the courage to stand up for them.

Field independence is supported when we find an opening to achieve our moral purposes. Sometimes these openings are difficult to see; but when one door closes (or an opportunity appears to be lost), another door often opens.

How is it possible to find this opening? Our search is aided by engaging our imagination, exercising a degree of flexibility, self-reflection, and dialogue with trusted others. Perhaps what makes it easier to maintain our integrity and respond with honesty and moral courage is when we know the best practices in the areas we teach and when we maintain caring, respectful relationships with our students and colleagues. It is also beneficial to draw on our ability to communicate in respectful and nonthreatening ways.

When we complain about our work but make no effort to address the situation, this leads to a frustrating loop of gossip, irritation, and inaction. In such situations, we believe that no other options exist. If work is untenable and our integrity is compromised, and we see no possibility of changing the situation, it may be time to find some type of support or a different work situation. If there are no tenable options to leave our unhealthy work situation, another option might be to look for a mitigation strategy (such as the one adopted by the teacher in the following story) to minimize the damage to our students and ourselves.

> *As a kindergarten teacher I was very concerned that our young students experience their early years in school as ones that affirmed their gifts and assured them all that they were competent and capable human beings. I felt the only forms of testing that were appropriate to this end were informal ones that left no child exposed as someone who didn't know important things or as not being able to do something that others could do.*
>
> *Our director informed us that we were to use a standardized test to be administered twice a year to all kindergarten students. At the meeting where this was announced, I argued for evaluation practices that helped teachers develop students' strengths and fill their needs without such formal tests.*
>
> *At the end of the day, the standardized testing was adopted by administration but I felt that at least I had made my convictions known and that I backed my arguments with my experiences and suggested alternatives. I knew that many of my colleagues agreed with me and that we would administer the tests in the most sensitive way possible.*

In those situations where we feel ourselves being cramped into a small space with few options for actions in harmony with our integrity, our soul can be restored through turning to our imagination, creativity, self-compassion, and collegial network to find an opening that sheds new light on possibilities for action. And through these means, we may find the path that we can walk together, preserving our integrity and that of our colleagues.

Some Questions to Ask Are:

- What parts of myself, character, or personality contribute to my integrity?
- What personal virtues help me to maintain my integrity?

- What enables me to stand up for and act upon my beliefs and values?
- Is it possible to be partly honorable or have partial integrity?
- How does our teaching situation support our integrity? What supports are available in the school system to mitigate or change a situation where our integrity at the school level is compromised?

Some Practices to Consider Are:

- To preserve your integrity, consider your motivations before saying or doing something. For example, think about what virtues you are drawing upon and if your potential statement or action is meant to support a higher good or if it is subtly intended to deliver a "hidden" criticism in order to bolster your own self-righteousness or need to be "right."
- Notice when your emotions are not congruent with your words or actions, and look for the more constructive potential in the situation so that your actions reflect your feelings and convictions.
- Dialogue groups: With your collegial group, discuss scenarios that could be threats to teacher integrity. Take turns practicing clearly expressing how you feel about what you are observing as a potential threat to teachers acting on their beliefs and vision. Follow this by expressing what you need or value, and the concrete actions that could be taken to preserve your integrity.

Thoughts to Remember

Integrity stems from the Latin word "integer" whose root meaning is wholeness or completeness. We can say then that our integrity holds us together and keeps us authentic. We have a quality of being genuine and honorable because we act in accord with our moral principles and remain true to our values.

The question, "What is my intention or the good I mean to do as a teacher?" can help us to be clear about what is at stake when we choose a response to an administrative directive that violates our sense of what is right, helpful, and a support for learning. In those situations where decisions are made which we feel are not in the best interests of our students or us, our imagination, creativity, self-compassion, and collegial network are the assets that can help us find the best ways to work within the bounds of our integrity as a whole and caring person.

NOTE

1. Larrivee's (2012) research confirms this.

Chapter 10

Working Well with Curriculum Requirements

> *As I looked through the [arts education] curriculum I thought, "There are a lot of times [sample lessons in the curriculum] where students are just looking at the world around them and from different points of view. There's not always a product. It might just be having students look at things in a new way or having them experience something. Looking at the different ideas in the curriculum helped me to see that I had an idea in my head of what I think arts ed is – I always thought that I had to produce something."* (conversation with Rachel[1] in Thurgood Sagal, 2009, p. 60)

Despite her busy teaching life, Rachel consistently demonstrates an openness of spirit. This supports her in keeping an open mind to the curricula she works with and allows her to discover her informal theory regarding arts education and the development of products. As teachers, it is helpful to be familiar enough with the respective curricula that we work with so that we can discover and let go of any misconceptions, and find out what the various curriculum documents actually support.

In the excerpt above, it is clear that Rachel's focus in arts education has been to support student development of products. By becoming familiar with the curriculum and its contents, Rachel discovers that engaging students in processes (such as observing and talking about ideas that arise as part of learning in arts education) deepens their understanding, allows them to express their ideas in individual and novel ways, and strengthens their ability to problem solve within the creative process. Rachel felt enriched by the ideas and engagement of her students. When a well thought-out curriculum is approached with an open mind, greater learning for everyone is often the reward.

We can all question our attitude to any requirement from state, province, or local authority. Do we tend to dismiss them as restrictions on our professional freedom or examine the nature of the regulation, policy, or curriculum document first before deciding how to respond? A good question to ask if we find our tendency is to become defensive is, "Am I trying to protect some part of myself from this form of restriction?"

A new curriculum can arouse an array of responses. Teachers, like all humans, develop patterns in the ways they respond to any form of authority. Perhaps some of us have not lost a tendency to rebel against almost any restriction – a tendency that we had as teenagers. Others may be passive or submissive to authority without questioning whether a requirement is in students' best interest. In some cases, our resistance to a new curriculum or program may come from our levels of stress and not from the curriculum. Self-knowledge of what is behind our response to new requirements is always beneficial.

Other aspects of self-knowledge are important in finding ways to evaluate a curriculum or program. It is constructive to review our personal philosophy of teaching, learning, and relating well to students. It may also be worthwhile to know our informal theory of education and view of the state of knowledge in a subject area. Do we understand, for example, that history can be viewed from the perspective of a soldier or a member of parliament? Do we see knowledge of physics as open-ended with new findings emerging all the time?

These reflections will help us to evaluate a curriculum for its fit with our present understanding. We are then in a better position to see the strengths or weaknesses of new curricula, programs, or resources. Perhaps they will present opportunities for new learning or professional growth, even a kind of rejuvenation as our interest in an area of study is rekindled. Can we find that open, balanced response that inquires with genuine interest into the contents and meaning of a document or policy? This openness is an essential aspect of the teaching profession – one that we try to model for our students.

One way to open our mind to explorations of mandated curricula and recommended resources is to imagine how demanding it would be if we were to develop a curriculum for each subject area ourselves. We may discover more ways in which curricula can save us planning time and, similar to Rachel, enrich our understanding of important aspects of teaching in a particular field of study. In the majority of cases, curricula have been developed by persons with a depth of knowledge and a passion for a particular subject. Curriculum developers usually have the time that we don't to investigate a range of teaching methods that support learning in the area of knowledge of focus.

It is also the case that some programs and curricula are developed or influenced by special interest groups to reflect a certain value system or set of beliefs that are not reflective of cultural diversity or congruent with democratic principles. In these situations, the mandated curricula tend to be narrow in ways that don't allow for students' interests, questions, critical thinking, and creativity. They also may not support teacher professionalism but rather be restrictive in ways that is sometimes called "teacher-proof."

Our children and teenagers are such a precious resource that even under circumstances such as administrative curriculum directives which we feel are not in students' best interests, or situations of resource shortages and restrictions, we can look for ways and supports to continue to teach in keeping with our deepest beliefs. As classroom teachers, we are knowledgeable about our students and their unique learning needs and, therefore, in the strongest position to determine how best to work with curriculum requirements.

To work well with mandated curricula and other requirements such as particular forms of testing or the use of specific resources, it is helpful to have confidence in our abilities to adapt our approach to best meet students' needs while supporting their success in relation to the particular requirements. It is also fruitful to keep up to date in relation to promising practices in the relevant subject area. This knowledge gives us confidence and supports our abilities to incorporate new practices and evaluate curricula from an informed base. It is also our devotion to our students that will help us find a workable solution.

When our school district mandated a program that was not accommodating the needs of my students, I took the program home and read it thoroughly so I could see the concepts and skills that the program was promoting. Then, I used my knowledge of my students and best practices to help my students understand the concepts and practise the skills of the new programme in developmentally appropriate ways.

In other situations, trust in the good intentions of administrators and colleagues can help us find respectful responses.

When I arrived at the school during the summer, I made a point to talk to the principal about why I wanted wires strung across my Elementary Level classroom ceiling to display student art work and writing. During the month of September, I periodically brought student drawings with their hand-printed descriptions into the principal's office while positively exclaiming over students' attempted phonetic spellings of difficult words – noting what students had learned in that regard and pointing out how we could see their growth in capturing ideas (and in spelling) over the days and weeks. In this way, I helped my principal to understand developmentally appropriate practice in relation to my Grade 1 students.

Despite perceived or real restrictions that come from compulsory programs and tests, there are always some important life lessons that you can teach without taking time away from curriculum obligations. We teach who we are. We are the main curriculum for our students in terms of learning better and worse ways to treat others. When we talk respectfully to all students, when we consistently show how we care for our students through our speech and behaviors, we are helping them learn to support others. It is this "hidden" curriculum that colors all aspects of student learning.

The personal support we offer to individual students also helps to teach them that they are good and worthy just as they are. The ways that we demonstrate our belief that all of them can learn and grow gives them faith in themselves. When we show through our enthusiasm, interest, and curiosity our own genuine love of a particular subject matter or phenomenon, we are teaching that learning is enjoyable and life-enriching. It's hard to imagine a more positive curriculum than the one we are creating through our way of being in the classroom and the world.

Relevance to students' lives is one of the greatest assets we can bring to our teaching. Our own interest and passion for learning in any given subject area are also gifts we bring to our teaching. In thinking about what the school system requires us to teach, we can use our imagination and creativity to connect this subject matter and skill teaching to what interests the students, what they care about, and what they feel they need to know to solve problems in their lives.

Some Questions to Ask Are:

- Do I know my own tendencies and usual attitudes to any new curricula, policy, or regulation?
- Is there something in my nature that seeks the security of the familiar? Do I know where this need comes from and whether it is holding me back from openness to new learning?
- Do curricula support student voice? In what ways? Can I add further supports for student input and leadership? Can I take advantage of curricular topics to encourage students' critical and creative thinking?
- What am I teaching by my way of relating to students? What learning do I see resulting from the kind of role model I am?
- How can we adopt a positive approach to implementing new curricula in ways that meet all students' needs and what additional knowledge and abilities do we need to acquire?

Some Practices to Consider Are:

- Take some time to reflect on your attitudes to new curricula, assessment tools, or other requirements. When your initial response is usually negative,

do you know what is behind that response? Consider your strengths as a teacher and see if you can find ways to believe in your abilities to learn new things and to use the requirements to grow as a teacher and a person.
- Read through the various curricula and consider how you can design experiences that will grab students' interest, touch their spirit, and be relevant to their daily lives.
- Dialogue groups: Work with your colleagues or teacher network to develop personal-professional growth plans that involve an important step in implementing a particular curriculum. (See Appendix C.) Make a list of supports you will need and changes that would help you achieve your goals. Seek administrative support.[2]

Thoughts to Remember

We can look at curriculum requirements as restrictions or as guides. Our view may have partly to do with our usual way of responding to new requirements. It is helpful to know our patterns in this regard and the needs that underlie them. In order to get the most out of curricula in each subject area we teach, it is beneficial to review them with an inquiring attitude – one that is interested in any new content or methods they contain. In most cases, they will enrich our understanding of a subject area and ways to teach it.

In supporting students' learning, the mandated curriculum is one tool, our knowledge of our students is another, our pedagogical expertise is a third, and a fourth (and powerful curriculum) is the kind of role model we are in terms of caring and respectful ways of relating with others and showing genuine interest in a subject area. Using all four ways to support students' growth results in authentic and lasting learning for everyone.

NOTES

1. Rachel is a pseudonym for the teacher who is talking in this curriculum study.

2. Ideas in this section are based on *Classroom Curriculum Connections* (Saskatchewan Education, 2001).

Chapter 11

Strengthening Our Resilience

> The minute I was far enough above the town to see I could make the towhead, I begun to look sharp for a boat to borrow, and the first time the lightning showed me one that warn't chained I snatched it and shoved. It was a canoe, and warn't fastened with nothing but a rope. The towhead was a rattling big distance off, away out there in the middle of the river, but I didn't lose no time; and when I struck the raft at last I was so fagged I would "a" just laid down to blow and gasp if I could afforded it.
>
> —Mark Twain

But Huck Finn knew that he did not have time to "blow and gasp." So he called out to Jim to wake up and set the raft loose. They had been floating down the river on a raft, enjoying adventures and narrowly escaping life-threatening mishaps on the way. Throughout Mark Twain's novel *Adventures of Huckleberry Finn*, Huck consistently demonstrates his resilience by surviving an abusive father, a well-meaning Miss Watson, some wily tricksters, and Tom Sawyer's "sage" advice. It is refreshing to see how Huck continues to draw upon his resilience when others, in similar situations, may have given up.

Through literature, we see how fictional characters survive hardships and how they deal with their emotions in tough situations. Can their strategies inform our own life and strengthen our own resolve when facing difficult situations? While we may find some of Huck's antics to be outlandish, we can appreciate his strong spirit. When considered in relation to our own lives, his refusal to give up and be overtaken by negative or destructive events is worth noting.

Resilience is the ability to readily recover from a variety of challenges. A resilient person believes that he or she is strong enough to recover from great pain and loss as well as from the stressful events of daily life. This belief develops incrementally over our lifetime as we discover our ability for resiliency with each age and stage of our life. Resilience comes from spiritual strength – thus all the attitudes and activities that feed the spirit help to build resilience.

As a helping profession, teaching requires resilience as it involves the challenge of addressing our feelings and the ways we express them when dealing with others. When we are not genuine, or can't control anger and frustration, this can deplete our energy and, if we're not careful, decrease our resilience and sense of self-efficacy. It is important, then, to express our emotions in ways that are in tune with who we are, to conserve our energy reserve and to shore up or build our resilience.

It is sometimes helpful to see how our emotions may rise to protect ourselves in some way. For example, while I might feel the emotion of anger, is it possible that the anger is rising in me because I am afraid of something? If so, it might be more important to focus on restoring my sense of safety rather than being swallowed up by an ever-widening circle of anger. Reflecting on what we may be protecting when we feel an emotion may allow us to discover something new. Anger and defensiveness can be the result of an underlying need that is not being fulfilled and is another focus for our reflections.

Larrivee (2012) recommends interacting with positive colleagues to counteract emotional exhaustion. The story below demonstrates an experienced teacher's reflection regarding this.

> *It is difficult at times not to get sucked into the vortex of negativity that can come with any workplace. I make very conscious efforts to surround myself with the people with a positive frame of mind about our profession. This was quite difficult as a new teacher and, even 22 years in, I feel I have to consciously make the effort at times not to get drawn in. I also work with my kids [students] on this regarding who they surround themselves with. Who we choose to interact with has such an effect on our experiences, our thoughts and how we choose to progress.*

Beginning teachers appreciate the efforts of their more experienced peers in offering them understanding and timely, practical advice before a problem related to their inexperience becomes unmanageable. Such interactions and advice can build the resilience of those new to teaching by providing emotional support along with strategies to deal with and recover from challenging events and situations. In a way, novice and experienced teachers alike develop greater resilience from knowing that others care about their challenges, understand their realities, and are happy to offer support.

When we are faced with a challenging situation, it is not only useful to consider the effort required to respond, it is also helpful to consider if it is possible to view the situation differently. For Larrivee (2012), "the important point is to raise your awareness and understanding of what is happening, to acknowledge your feelings, and to explore alternative ways of thinking, and ultimately, feeling" (p. 60).

Exploring alternative ways of thinking is not to be confused with dwelling on or over-thinking a situation. Rather, the focus is to consider if there is a different way to view a particular situation. Another aspect of being resilient under duress is that of being able to see positive aspects of difficult situations, perhaps not immediately but before a downward spiral has overtaken us for a lengthy period (Fredrickson, 2009). It is helpful to remind ourselves in times of adversity, "I may bend, but I won't break."

By staying aware during a distressing situation, we can consider if an act was intentional and how much control we have in moderating the situation. Our responses can draw upon our energy to *compose* ourselves rather than fall into habitual patterns that may create anxiety, which, in turn, lowers our resilience. We can also look for the deeper meaning behind disruptive situations. Is there a learning opportunity that presents itself? Treating challenging situations as an opportunity to search for the hidden or underlying meaning can inform our response and support our ability to recover with grace.

One of the ways to strengthen resilience is to have strong sources of meaning in our life.[1] Meaning is created both by having an overarching sense of purpose for our life and also smaller sources of meaning that enrich every day. These can be simple things like smelling our first cup of coffee in the morning, feeling sunlight coming in our window and warming our face, watching the flames in a fireplace or campfire, or seeing a smile on a student's face when they succeed at something.

A way to tap into these sources of meaning is to activate them through our imagination. Visualized meaningful moments have been shown to have a relaxing effect and increase our sense of well-being. If we don't have time for a cup of coffee on a particular morning when rushing to school, perhaps we can visualize how good it will smell when we have our first morning break.

Scientists in the field of positive psychology[2] have made many contributions to understanding and strengthening resilience. One of these is the focus on knowing and acting on your character strengths and virtues, which include strengths such as creativity, open-mindedness, moral courage, fairness, feeling gratitude, and appreciating beauty. Findings in this area demonstrate that successful and happy people both know and act on their strengths.[3]

Developing greater understanding of personal strengths is especially valuable to people in the helping professions such as teaching. Knowing our own character strengths helps us to recognize and show appreciation for those of our students and colleagues, thus building their resilience. Knowledge of our particular character strengths gives us confidence in relation to the strengths we know we have and may also prompt us to think about what other character strengths we might want to develop.

Regularly acknowledging our contributions at work also builds resilience and helps us leave school each day with our spirit refreshed. Taking a moment at the end of the school day to quietly reflect and focus on our accomplishments can become an integral part of our daily routine. Feeding the spirit in this way strengthens our resilience and supports us in pursuing our teaching practice with passion.

Some Questions to Ask Are:

- What challenges have I overcome as a result of my resilience and how has this further bolstered my ability to be resilient?
- What sources of meaning in my life contribute to my resilience?
- What strategies have I used to feed my spirit in order to strengthen my resilience, particularly when externally imposed stresses are ongoing?
- How can I help my emotions to slow down, give me the message, and then move on? For example, when I am feeling sad, can I focus on why the sadness is there and what it might be trying to protect (e.g., my self-esteem)? Once I know what is being protected, I can consider what must be restored.
- What models of resilience in life, literature, and film have we been inspired by and how have they helped us build our resilience?

Some Practices to Consider Are:

- Develop a daily habit of creating a positive state of mind as a way to bolster your resilience. For example, each morning, greet the day as a blessed, abundant one. Alternatively, each evening before falling asleep, foresee the restful and refreshing sleep that you will have.
- Take the time to reflect on what makes your life meaningful and act to incorporate more possibilities to create meaning into your days and weeks, as a strategy to increase your sense of well-being and strengthen your resilience.
- Dialogue groups: With your colleagues, discuss how to bolster each other's resilience when external forces are negatively affecting your teaching climate on an ongoing basis.

Thoughts to Remember

We are stronger than we think. While we need to be resilient in the face of the uncertainty, pace, and sometimes uncontrollable classroom events, this way of being is possible for us. A good starting point for strengthening resilience is to learn about and use our character strengths.

We can recover and sustain resilience in many other ways including how we look for the positive in a stressful situation, develop many sources of meaning in life, and nourish our spirit. Resilience is strengthened when emotional and spiritual needs are met. The heart of these practices is belief in our ability to learn, grow, and change.

NOTES

1. Frederickson's (2009) research confirms this.
2. See Frederickson (2009), Lyubomirsky (2013), Peterson and Seligman (2004), and Seligman (2011).
3. Tests that help you to discover your character strengths and information about ways to further develop them are available online at no cost, including at www.authentichappiness.org and the website of the Values in Action nonprofit institute www.viacharacter.org.

Chapter 12

Using Technology Wisely

> People scoring high on meaningfulness scales perceive themselves as living life with purpose, fulfillment, and satisfaction, and do not feel socially isolated. Meaningfulness is a marker of social connectivity, not social media connectivity. (Selhub & Logan, 2012, p. 227)

There are many positive ways to use our new and old technological media. Teachers can communicate with colleagues around the world, read blogs on educational topics of interest, and write their own. Research for both teachers and students is often simplified by search engines such as Google. Computers and smart boards can bring images, sounds, and experiences to the classroom that strengthen lessons in ways that books, chalkboards, and lectures cannot. Email and social media such as Skype help us stay connected to friends and family when we can't be with them in person.

With all the benefits, it is also good to stand back from your own media practices to ask the questions, "Are there also losses when technological media are used to replace direct contact with others and the natural world, or live performances and field trips? How much time in front of a screen is too much? Are there physical, psychological, and social concerns that result from media use?" We feel these are important questions to ask and offer you the results of the growing body of research in this area.

Selhub and Logan (2012) describe research and observations from scientists, psychologists, and medical doctors that throw light on some of the negative effects of excessive time spent in front of computers, including increased stress, overstimulation, information overload, fatigue, and reduction in physical activity and social interaction. As well, there are health hazards that result from the types of waves that our media technology and microwaves give off.

The brains of young children are particularly vulnerable to damage from the electromagnetic frequency radiation from cell phones (Beresford-Kroeger, 2013).

The term Internet and Digital Device Addiction are becoming increasingly used to describe people who have real difficulty not being "connected" at all times and become restless or agitated if not interacting with their media. Research is showing that many children and teenagers are becoming addicted to computer games and that many of these are based in violence (Harris, 2014).[1] Many people feel the effects of being at work 24/7 and losing more and more leisure time. Time spent on the computer and with social media takes time away from opportunities for reflection and personal growth as well as from rest and renewal.

Kabat-Zinn (2005) questions if, as a result of our constant connectedness to others and to work via our cell phones and other technology, we are losing this connection to our own bodies and our inner life.

> Are we becoming so connected to everybody else that we are never where we really are? We are at the beach on the cell phone, so are we there? We are walking down the street on the cell phone, so are we there? We are driving on the cell phone, so are we there? Do we have to let the possibility of being in our life go out the window in the face of the speedup in our pace of life and the possibilities for instant connection? (p. 153)

Research has shown a significant correlation between high computer use and a lessening of empathy and understanding of others.[2] Emails and text messages allow us to present the self we *want* to be but not necessarily who we are. With these forms of communication, we can't see the accompanying body language or hear the emphases or emotional tone in the speaker's voice. We miss all the ways that people show their feelings in their eyes, or when they are hesitating to say something, or what mood they were in when they sent the text. The loss may be a lessening awareness of the effect and influence we have on one another.

In some ways, we are also losing authenticity as a value and a virtue. You can say anything in a text message. You can abbreviate your thoughts but have great difficulty expressing the more subtle feelings and experiences that reveal your uniqueness and create intimacy. These might include the glimmers of anxiety you are feeling or your momentary experiences of the beauty and poignancy of being alive and human.

You may become less and less aware of your own body and how it is feeling, your soul and what it is longing for, and less able to sit with yourself in silence and solitude. The sensing and feeling and deeper thinking that render life meaningful are not easily communicated to those you care about through digital means. They require presence and time and meandering conversations where each of you is seeing how thoughts and emotions pass over faces and affect the quality and mood of the relationship.

Fortunately for teachers, their work life is spent in relationships with real students and personal and professional interactions with their students and colleagues. It is perhaps as much for our students' sake as for our own that it is helpful to be aware of the pitfalls and weaknesses of new information technologies as well as the rewards. While fostering discussions with this focus, we can support our students' critical thinking abilities and raise our own awareness of the differences between activities like texting and sending emails as opposed to being with our friends and family members. We can also create lessons that help students to understand the immeasurable damage caused by cyber-bullying and best ways to respond to any they receive or witness.

Technologies are neither good nor bad, but they aren't neutral. Their potential for damage or benefit stems from the ways they are used. We need to be aware of the time we spend digitally connected and how to use the Internet wisely in our personal and professional life. We can enrich the learning, even the democracy and fairness of our teaching, through supplementing lessons with images, videos, and educational courses available online.

When we access online courses, no one knows our family history, our weight, or our previous schooling experiences and results. Students who are struggling can be helped by online courses that impart knowledge in a step-by-step manner, where feedback on the quality or accuracy of their understanding is given individually. This means their success or failure to understand is private and lessens the competitiveness prevalent in many classroom situations. As well, virtual learning offers shy students the opportunity to participate in online discussions and chats.

Online learning is convenient and flexible regarding time and location. Courses can be offered anytime and anywhere. This allows us and our students to better fit teaching and learning into personal schedules within a comfortable learning environment. Technology offers us greater access to expertise without the constraints of travel and related costs. We can access a broad spectrum of relevant content and interact with fellow students, colleagues, and instructors through chat, discussion thread, or email without waiting for the school door to open.

This is especially enriching for smaller schools or communities. Is there really someone on staff who has the expertise to teach calculus or specific science courses, or any of the arts? Is there a local anthropologist or mechanic whom students can readily approach for a class project? If not, they are likely to be found online.

One of the biggest benefits is making connections with learners of similar interests in other parts of the world. One teacher comments on her experience, *"It was not only the discussions with people who are studying and discussing the same ideas, but relating them to very different community and cultural situations. We learn so much from each other!"* Teachers who want to create learning groups can really benefit from establishing online connections.

While technological connections allow us to learn about others and the world, and develop rewarding relationships by interacting with a range of individuals from a wide variety of backgrounds and locations; we also benefit from stretches of solitude. The poet William Wordsworth, who spent so much time walking the moors of the Lake District in England, understood that the one need of the spirit to return us to our essential self requires leaving the busy world behind. And yet, his world did not contain the pace nor distractions of ours. These lines from his poem, *The Prelude*, express this need for quiet stretches of time alone:

When from our better selves we have too long
Been parted by the hurrying world, and droop,
Sick of its business, of its pleasures tired,
How gracious, how benign is Solitude.

Perhaps we need this time alone to face ourselves, to question if we are living as we intended and being the teacher we wanted to be.

The more we are engrossed with the outer world available through the new information technologies, the more we may need the counter balance of activities that calm the nervous system and bring us into greater awareness of what's happening in our lives and what emotional and spiritual needs we may not be meeting. With awareness, we can use social media and information technologies to enrich our lives and also continue to live a full life of direct contact with the world.

Some Questions to Ask Are:

- How is my use of information technologies influencing the moment-to-moment choices of how I live my life and how I teach in the classroom?
- For what purposes do I usually use the computer? In what ways does it contribute to making me a better teacher or a better person?
- How can I strengthen my classroom practice through the use of technology?
- How can I increase the authenticity of relationships in an online learning environment?
- How aware are we of the damage our students may be facing by their use of digital devices? What could we do as a staff to raise the awareness of students and parents in relation to the physical and mental health hazards of overuse of social media and computer games, along with their risk of digital device addictions?

Some Practices to Consider Are:

- Make a commitment to yourself to slow down the pace of your life away from school by dedicating time to being technology free. For at least 15 minutes every day, take time to go for a walk, stretch the tight muscles in your body, or sit quietly and just pay attention to your breath. When on vacation, do not access technology for work-related reasons.
- Develop your awareness of ways to use your technology to support your connection to others and the natural world when you can't be there in person.
- Dialogue groups: In a teacher dialogue group or among staff, reflect upon the ways your students use computer technologies and plan a set of lessons together that raise awareness of both their potential benefits and harm. You might also investigate if there is equitable computer access across the families in your school community.

Thoughts to Remember

We can benefit from the connections, to people we care about, that social media offers us. We can enrich our lives and those of our students through access to Internet sites that bring the world into the classroom with full color and sound or provide structured independent learning opportunities for those who need them. It is important as well to share and discuss with our students findings from the growing body of research into the threats to health and overall well-being posed by the overuse of the Internet and digital devices.

Important questions to ask from time to time about our use of these technologies are: "How can technology be used to broaden my students' understanding of the world? How can I use technology to enhance my personal life?" When using technology, it is important to ask as well, "Is it time for a break? What else could I be doing right now that would better meet the needs of my body, mind, and soul?" Using technology wisely means not just asking these questions but also acting on them.

NOTES

1. Harris' (2014) book, *The End of Absence: Reclaiming What We've Lost in a World of Constant Connection*, is a good source of this rather disturbing research.
2. Selhub and Logan (2012) summarize the findings of a number of studies that confirm this loss.

Chapter 13

Reducing Our Stress

"Get to your places!" shouted the Queen in a voice of thunder, and people began running about in all directions, tumbling up against each other; however, they got settled down in a minute or two, and the game began.
    Alice thought she had never seen such a curious croquet-ground in all her life; . . . the croquet balls were live hedgehogs, and the mallets live flamingoes, and the soldiers had to double themselves up and to stand on their hands and feet, to make the arches.

—Lewis Carroll

Similar to how Alice felt when she was swept up in the Queen's curious game of croquet in Wonderland, there are times when teaching can feel like the ground is shifting under our feet. School district policies or school-level decisions can affect our teaching life in unforeseen ways. Even our best-laid plans, developed through hours of careful thought and based on current research, can be destroyed within minutes. To withstand stressors that enter our teaching day, it is important to develop a repertoire of strategies to alleviate stress.

Eastern philosophies such as Buddhism and Taoism develop their support for the suffering of humans from the understanding that everything is connected to everything else and everything is in a process of constant change. Physicists and cosmologists agree. From these insights, they describe the ways in which so much of the stress we suffer comes from seeing ourselves as separate and able to control that which is not ultimately controllable.

Remembering that everything changes and ends, that "this too shall pass," helps us when caught in a stressful situation. A strong practice for teachers which stems from these understandings is that of letting go of our tight need to be in control all the time and of all aspects of classroom life. This is a form of rigidity that is common to all of us but calls for a more flexible and fluid approach in our thinking and in our actions.[1]

> *When arts education was introduced as a Required Area of Study in our jurisdiction, I was worried about my ability to teach all four strands of the arts – in particular, dance. I had experienced 12 years of instruction in math, language arts, social studies, the sciences, and other areas but I had not experienced dance as a student. Therefore, I had very little context for my new teaching assignment and no previous role models to draw upon. After three weeks of struggling on my own, I asked a colleague who was an arts ed major to watch my next dance lesson and give me some pointers.*
>
> *As we chatted about my lesson after school, my colleague's immediate response was, "Why are you making all of the decisions for your students? They are capable of making some of the decisions regarding dance sequences on their own once you set the stage and the expectations." This caused me to think about my need to control the process when, instead, I should be focusing on the outcome. This realization had implications for how I taught in all areas of study – very eye opening for me.*

Often, it is our thoughts that need changing as much as it is the situation – in particular, we need to rebut any self-critical thoughts that undermine our confidence. Wimberger (2014) and scientists of brain research find that neurosculpting – repeated thought patterns that influence the growth of specific neural cells – eventually leads to the brain rewiring itself. As an experiment, try choosing one positive thought about yourself and think about it for a minute. Do this three times a day – perhaps on waking, after work, and before bed. See how your week unfolds as you choose a different positive aspect of yourself to reflect upon for the day.

A starting point for understanding the thought patterns that cause us stress is to increase our awareness of feelings of anxiety and their causes, and to notice when we are caught in a web of worries. While worry and anxiety are forms of thinking about past or future events which increase our distress; they are also common patterns of human behavior. It is difficult to simply *will* ourselves out of these behaviors. Excessive worry and anxiety can be debilitating and those who suffer from them require self-compassion and the support of understanding others. With greater awareness and knowledge of stress-reducing practices, we can adopt behaviors that lessen our stress and increase our well-being.

Worry and anxiety can be helpful signposts as they make us aware of where our energy is being directed. This allows us to tune into our body – a source of important knowledge. While it is not easy to move out of the spiral of anxiety, it is possible to engage in calming processes such as deep breathing and focusing on the task at hand in order to slow down the anxiety vortex.

Textbox 13.1   A Short Guide to Stress-Reduction

1. Nature is a great stress reducer as it brings us closer to our roots.
2. Humor can be another way to break out of our worrying.
3. Sometimes a colleague, friend, or family member can help us see the funny side of a worry by exaggerating it.
4. Finding "downtime" in our day can help alleviate stress and refresh our spirit.
5. Physical exercise gets us out of our heads and lessens our anxious thoughts.
6. Using positive visualizations of ourselves being successful and happy lowers anxiety.
7. Increasing our awareness of things we are grateful for decreases our stress.

For example, when faced with a stressful event, take seven deep breaths. With each breath, breathe out stress and breathe in fresh air expanding your chest and inner airways. Notice how you feel after this deep breathing. Use this practice as soon after a stressful experience as you can.

While we do not have control over events that have already happened, we can embrace the opportunity to learn from these events and choose to respond differently should they occur in the future. A practical response to worry is to act to alleviate its source; for example, paying that overdue bill. Another helpful practice we can adopt when we recognize that we are caught in the web of worries or anxiety is to turn our energies to a physical task that gets us out of our head and into our body. More helpful practices are shown in Textbox 13.1.

Vanslyke-Briggs (2010) suggests creating a stress journal or diary in order to note stressful events and what occurred before the stressful reaction was noticed. In this way, habitual patterns may be recognized and intervention strategies employed. She also provides a variety of healthy ways to respond to stress such as walking or talking with a supportive individual, or reframing understanding of the event. Sometimes it is helpful to mentally describe what you are seeing and hearing, as a way to hold your emotions at arm's length, while you attempt to make sense of the situation before responding.

Having a personal life where we feel relaxed, nurtured, and valued helps us to withstand significant amounts of stress. When we feel nurtured and supported by our family and friends, challenges feel more manageable. It is often our social support network that "prevents stress from knocking us down and getting in the way of achieving our goals" (Achor, 2010, p. 122). If we suffer from worry and anxiety in ways that are debilitating, we might consider seeking help from a counselor. Appendix B is a support for the practice of transforming the thinking that discourages us and this can also be used to help us assess how realistic our worries are.

Stress can also be reduced by adopting positive strategies such as finding something to look forward to or visualizing ourselves being successful. What we spend our time focusing on often ends up becoming our reality. Achor (2010) reminds us that "constantly scanning the world for the negative comes with a great cost. It undercuts our creativity, raises our stress levels, and lowers our motivation and ability to accomplish goals" (p. 46). Focusing on the negative predisposes us to perceive and heighten our awareness of the negative aspects of people and situations. This increases our stress and requires a lot of energy that could be directed elsewhere.

It is informative to make a list of the good things in your career and in your life, and consider how they help you to withstand stress. Practicing gratitude has been shown to lead to lower levels of stress hormones.[2] Similar to love and empathy, gratitude creates a biochemical shift in the body and can alter the physical activity of the brain. The brain responds to positive input and sends life-enhancing messages to every cell in the body. When we show gratitude for the good things in our life, we lower our stress levels and increase our health. Expressing our gratitude to the people who have made our life better contributes to our self-care as does showing more sympathy, less judgment, and greater appreciation for life itself. If we focus on our adventures, relaxing moments, and connections, our stress will fall away.

Establishing transitional spaces (such as reading a novel on the public transit system when heading home after work or taking time to make a journal entry before leaving school) can help us move from one environment to another and leave our stress behind. As we relax listening to the radio on our drive home from school, we allow our busy school day to fall away from us. This transitional strategy nurtures our spirit and refreshes us for our arrival home.

It is worth noting that some levels of stress are helpful if they heighten our awareness and lead to greater preparedness so that we can perform at our best (e.g., when preparing for an exam or a public-speaking engagement). While we can't eliminate stress from our lives, we can adopt behaviors that lessen its grip.

Some Questions to Ask Are:

- Is this a stressful time in my life? How can I use my awareness of the stress I am feeling to treat myself with the kindness I would like from others?
- What triggers a stress response for me? Is my need to control contributing to my stress level?

- Are there self-critical thoughts that I engage in which are contributing to my stress? (Refer to Appendix B to develop greater awareness of thought patterns and ways to transform self-critical thinking.)
- How can I restore a positive state of mind after a stressful event occurs?
- What actions can we take to reduce the stress levels at our school – for our students and for ourselves?

Some Practices to Consider Are:

- Analyse your stress triggers and current responses to stress. Notice if there is a pattern, and plan ahead for healthy ways to respond.
- Pay attention to physical cues such as talking fast, shortness of breath, clenching your teeth, or raising your voice. Internally acknowledge these cues as a signal for you to take a moment to lower your stress.
- Dialogue groups: With your colleagues, develop a debriefing process at the school level for teachers to access after a stressful event occurs.

Thoughts to Remember

Unpredictable, unpleasant, or sad events are a part of life. They need not debilitate us, however. We can learn to think differently about the stressors in our life and develop strategies that alleviate our stress and improve our overall well-being. An important starting place is to believe in our abilities to recover from troubling experiences and to recognize and change patterns of behavior that maintain our anxiety.

We can reflect on the nature of the stressful situations in our life, look for patterns, and develop healthier ways to respond. Becoming more aware of ways in which we view life through a negative lens, and using the energy this takes to increase our positivity is an important part of reducing stress. A set of beneficial practices include noting what we are grateful for each day, going for more walks, using our humor and creativity to turn things around, and becoming more fully in the moment.

NOTES

1. See Appendix B for support for other ways to increase our flexibility and reduce stress.
2. See McCraty, Barrios-Choplin, Rozman, Atkinson, and Watkins (1998).

Chapter 14

Harmonizing Our Personal and Professional Lives

"Kanyu," an ancient term for feng shui, means "Raise the head and observe the sky above; lower the head and observe the environment around us." A graphic portrayal of this philosophy is seen in ikebana, the Japanese art of flower arranging, which emphasizes form and balance. Here, the upper branch of the traditional arrangement represents heaven, the lower branch earth, and the line in between humans – the balance point between and the blending of heaven and earth. The goal of feng shui is to bring harmony and balance among the influx of heaven and earth energies and their influences on human lives. (Gerecht, 1999, p. 12)

The notion of harmony and balance in the practice of feng shui provides an interesting backdrop for thinking about our personal and professional lives. How is it possible in our busy day-to-day lives to attain this balance and to bring harmony between the energies of our teaching life, and our home and social lives? Attention to our energy level is important as work-related stress can lead to burnout if we are unable to protect our well-being.

As teachers, we want to be prepared for our interaction with students, even if this means taking time at home to plan for our school day. We also want to follow up on various things that have occurred during the school day even if this delays our arrival back home. This need to be competent, caring, and fulfill other aspects of our professional lives requires time that is difficult to find within the 24 hours of our day. It helps if we are mindful of the toll that this commitment takes on our personal lives and take steps to nurture our well-being.

It would be very stressful to be two different people, one at school and one at home. This divide may happen when we believe our identity as teachers has more worth than who we are outside of our school life. The value system of the society we live in often feeds on this inequality of perceptions of worth, making it easier to become tied up in and defined by our work. It is natural to want recognition from others for our teaching and the ways we strive to continuously improve. It may be harder to give ourselves recognition for being a good human being – a person of fundamental worth in our personal lives as well.

A shift in seeing our worth as coming from who we are most essentially as a human and not solely from the professional roles we play could help us remain whole and more balanced. Perhaps this recognition could help us have the same dedication to our personal well-being as we have for our professional competence. By embracing the energies of our personal and professional lives as the same person, we can better bring harmony into being.

It is particularly important for teachers who are highly engaged to protect their well-being by developing the commitment to regularly detach from work to renew their energy level. Recharging our "batteries" requires that we engage in activities unrelated to work. One helpful strategy is to build some type of exercise (such as an early morning bike ride, swimming at noon, or taking the dog for a walk after evening dinner) into our daily schedule, similar to how we book time for appointments or meetings. In this way, exercise is built into our day and becomes something that we do without thinking. This is a small commitment that we can make to protect and enhance our personal well-being.

Another helpful practice is to incorporate periodic "no-bag" days into our routine. No school work is taken home that day so that the evening or weekend can truly be devoted to family, friends, and other personal interests. A way to accomplish this is to have a repertoire of classroom activities to use at such times – ones that involve real learning but require no further preparation. When we do take work home (or work late at school), it is important to set a cut-off time. When the time arrives, the work is put away and our focus now moves to our personal lives. These strategies remind us to pay attention to our personal lives even though we may find our professional lives to be fulfilling.

In addition to building in daily commitments for wellness into our personal lives, it is equally important to pay attention to our body and the space surrounding it during our teaching day. With the busy and often rushed teaching day, it is easy to forget about basic bodily needs such as taking breaks, keeping hydrated, and chatting with a colleague. Conversely, it is easy to pay attention solely to our teaching life when we are surrounded by students' questions, needs, and joys. It is often our personal life that tends to suffer from inattention.

When we move beyond the practical level of ways to achieve a balance between our life at home and at school, the deeper challenges arise involving our emotions and spirit. We may understand the importance of letting go of concerns about work life and students so as not to let them disrupt our personal lives or deplete our energies further and at the same time accept that there are circumstances in which this is hard to do. When school concerns involve the suffering of one of our students, it is difficult to leave at the school door our sorrow about their situation.

While it is not always healthy to compartmentalize our lives, we can make an effort to set the worry aside until we can readdress it the next day at school. One way to do this would be to describe a concern from an incident at school or our heartache about a child we fear is being abused[1] and seek empathy and support from a loved one or close friend. This would entail a meaningful conversation and perhaps a hug, as opposed to an entire evening spent in despair.

As teaching is a career where we focus on the whole student and not solely on their intellectual development, our ability to help students face the many challenges in their lives, both inside and outside of school, depends not only on our expertise but also on our wholeness and on our energy level. Restoring and sustaining our energy level includes treating ourselves as whole individuals who are able to experience harmony and balance between activity and rest. In order to find clarity and create stability, we need to find the stillness at the center of our harmonic scale. Being centered and in harmony with the influences around us allows us to dedicate energy to students, family, and friends when they most need us.

Teachers experience all the joys and sorrows of human life, and the degree to which we can take in our experiences and truly feel them is partly the degree to which we can be present in the classroom to our students' realities. When a teacher suffers from the loss or illness of a family member or due to strife at home, the ability to stay emotionally balanced in the classroom can be very difficult.

> *When my marriage was failing, I felt myself to be increasingly fragile. At the same time, I expected to be able to perform well at school. I don't think I really understood the extent to which my nerves were frayed. One afternoon, I was talking to my class about some behaviours that I didn't want to see. I reminded them that I knew, and they knew, that they could do better. In those same moments, my emotions began to well up and I felt tears starting to form and flow down my face. I could see the distress my students felt immediately. I said to them, "There a number of things in my life right now that are sad – someone close to me died recently (which was true). This is not your fault, I know what good people you all are. I'm just a little tired and stressed. Let's take a minute to refocus by writing one sentence about something sad that happened in the novel you are reading."*

It isn't easy to prepare for the actualities of life; they can arise unexpectedly and are beyond our control like the tears of this teacher. We can seek support from those we trust, and do the practical things like trying to get more sleep or being sure to be well prepared with some straightforward lessons, but we are human. When there isn't harmony at home, or sad events happen, we don't need to go into detail with our students, but we do need to ensure that they don't feel responsible if we are shaken by our emotions. We also need to develop our emotional intelligence to the extent that we can, and know when we are feeling more stress than usual.[2]

In some situations, our work life can provide a lifeline when we have suffered a great loss. Coming to work provides an opportunity to lift ourselves out of the abyss of sorrow. Self-compassion can help us to recognize that the challenges of our personal life do color all of our life and, with this recognition, we can accept and let go of the need for perfection. We have to be "good enough" so that our students learn and grow from our time with them, but this doesn't mean smooth sailing every lesson or class period.

Finding a way to pay attention to our personal needs will, in the end, strengthen our commitment to addressing our professional needs. When teaching demands appear to be overwhelming, it is helpful to pause and consider how we can find time to address personal aspects of our life. While there is an art and a science to teaching, there is also an art and a science to integrating our personal and professional lives. In some ways, it involves working to meet the needs of the spirit at home and at school.

We can turn to our heart as the source of wisdom that enlightens us when our present balance is not serving us well. Attending with kindness to our personal and professional needs and interests contributes to our well-being while also providing a pathway to attaining harmony and balance in our lives. Attempting to find this pathway is a challenge that continues to shift and change throughout our working lives. Perhaps our goal, as noted by Gerecht in the opening quote, is as simple as being able to raise our head and "observe the sky above" and lower our head to "observe the environment around us" – a gentle practice of returning to the beauty of the world with an open heart.

Some Questions to Ask Are:

- What is the current balance between my personal life and my professional life?
- How can I maintain a focus on my whole being as a human with intellectual, social, emotional and spiritual needs both at school and at home?
- What would contribute to a greater sense of accomplishment in my professional life?
- What strategies would allow me to incorporate an appropriate and beneficial focus on my personal life within the busyness of my working career?
- Is there a way for us to start a new conversation about teachers' well-being, perhaps one that looks at a teacher's well-being more holistically including the needs of the spirit?

Some Practices to Consider Are:

- Think about personal activities that you enjoyed in the past, and which you enjoy in the present, and would like to enjoy in the future. Make a point to include some of these activities in your schedule in order to renew your energy level.
- Observe how often you engage in nourishing practices that lift your spirit and are health-giving (e.g., noticing butterflies, listening to music, drinking water). See if you can increase or broaden these practices.
- Dialogue groups: Hold a discussion with teaching colleagues about the challenges of balancing personal and professional lives. Use the four dimensions – physical, intellectual, social, and spiritual – to explore together and notice if any of the dimensions are particularly weak. Contribute ideas of adjustments that might be made in order to balance all four of them.

Thoughts to Remember

As we are whole beings, we need to take the needs of our bodies, minds, and spirits into account when trying to balance our personal and professional lives. Finding the delicate balance needed to participate fully each day requires self-compassion and the understanding that the well-being of those we care for depends to a great extent on our own well-being. Our participation will be affected by challenges, both personal and professional. At these times, we need self-care and the support of caring others. There are also many practical strategies we can use in achieving balance between the energy we expend on our teaching life and our personal or home life.

The practices of feng shui and flower arranging offer lovely metaphors for both seeing the sky, and smelling and tending the roses – reminding us that responsibilities need to be balanced by the rest and relaxation that are means to long-term well-being. We can use this same balance in the classroom integrating thinking time with breaks to stretch and look around, providing balance and harmony both for our students and for ourselves.

NOTES

1. Even when we have followed all the procedures related to a concern of this magnitude and support the student with our genuine care, our heartache does not end with these steps.

2. Appendices B and D describe practices that increase emotional intelligence and awareness of our thoughts, feelings, and tension in the body and ways to reduce stress.

Chapter 15

Creating Positive Energy in the Classroom

Sister Mary Elephant!

(General hubbub of students laughing and joking in classroom)

Voice of Teacher: Good morning, class. (Student noise continues)

Teacher (louder): Good morning, class! (Student noise continues)

Teacher (even louder): Class! (Noise continues) SHUT UP!!! (Noise stops)

Teacher (quietly): Thank you. As you know, your regular teacher Sister

Rosetta Stone is on a small vacation. However, she does send her love and these finger paintings and these dust cloths she is making. I am your substitute teacher Sister Mary Elephant. (Student noise starts up again)

Teacher (louder): Attention, class! (Noise continues) Class!! (Noise continues) SHUT UP!!!

Teacher (quietly): Thank you. Young man, now give me that knife.

(Cheech & Chong, 1970s)

If you ever hear the skit above, which wildly exaggerates a misbehaving class and a teacher's response, it will bring a smile to your lips. That is because of the visual picture that comes to mind when we hear the sweet and gentle Sister Mary Elephant screaming unceremoniously "Shut up!" and then meekly saying, "Thank you" in a tiny voice. This type of outrageously bizarre behavior is not, of course, expected or becoming of a nun (or anyone else for that matter).

It does serve to remind us of the extent to which our way of being either calms the classroom atmosphere and restores the focus on learning or contributes to a disturbed atmosphere. While many books help teachers with a range of advice in relation to classroom management, the emphasis here is on the way teachers' vision, values, sensitivity to the classroom energy, and other personal qualities support a classroom environment where everyone feels safe, valued, and able to contribute. Research shows that teacher stress is highly related to difficult student behavior, poor classroom climate, and overall classroom management.[1] Such stress is particularly noted in beginning teachers, but even experienced teachers look for ways to work effectively and compassionately with their students and build a community of competent and kind learners.

Creating positive energy begins with our vision, the legacy we want to leave with students as a teacher who cares about their overall well-being. We are helped by our clarity in relation to those teacher qualities that support a safe and warm classroom atmosphere. Our trustworthiness, fairness, sincerity, and kindness are qualities that create emotional safety and are worth maintaining as pillars of our vision. When our vision is also one of helping our students develop sensitivity to the classroom atmosphere and supporting them to respect and care about the learning of their classmates, responsibility for classroom climate is shared.

A vision is created out of values and it is helpful for us to reflect regularly on what we care most about in relation to our teaching. It is very human to feel we know what is important to us, yet act contrary to those values at times. For example, do we say we value individual progress but grade our students by one standard that measures them against their classmates? Competition and comparisons increase anxiety in the atmosphere. That is one reason to know our teaching values and continue to develop awareness of whether our students are learning and benefiting from them.

The positive atmosphere of the classroom is also dependent on the confidence we have that our wise heart will hold the environment calm and steady in most situations. So much of creating and maintaining this relatively serene atmosphere comes from our inner nature, our acceptance that everything will not always go as planned, and our belief that we can act well and restore a peaceful atmosphere. We can be more calm and confident because we trust the goodness at our center and the fundamental goodness of our students. We don't set rigid standards for behavior – our own or theirs. It is hard to teach calmness, but belief in our respectful behaviors and teaching competencies, and awareness of our emotions, body tension, and repetitive thoughts are good starting points.

Another teacher quality that contributes to a positive and healthy classroom atmosphere is a certain degree of humility, a lack of pride based in a need to be perfect. When we can accept ourselves as ordinary human beings, without a strong need to be better than others, it is much easier to maintain our equilibrium and sense of humor.

It is rare to have a class where all students are eager to learn and behave respectfully to you and their classmates. Most of us have taught challenging students and students can be challenging in ways that call on our ingenuity, patience, and understanding. Disruptive behaviors, withdrawn students, and students with disabilities all have needs that require thoughtful responses. The quality that can make a positive difference for a teacher is the ability to recognize when he or she needs help and to not feel diminished in any way by asking for it. Using the counselors, special education consultants, speech therapists, and your administrators as supports is a strength, not a weakness.

It is normal to feel a range of emotions including anxiety and anger when responding to a disruption of the learning or the behavior of one student who hurts another. It is the expression of this emotion that can restore the positive ethos of the classroom or further fuel the flames of the disruption. Can we respond during a difficult situation without raising our voice (like Sister Mary Elephant) or clenching our teeth? As we become aware of our bodily reaction, this may provide us with the time to "take a breath" and consider our response. Modeling responses that don't "ratchet up" a situation but instead calm the atmosphere are helpful for students to see and experience.

Students learn much from how we behave as teachers and measure our behavior against what we say. Honesty is an essential element of gaining and keeping their trust. Students are very sensitive to any lack of sincerity in our behavior. It is so important then, to do the work of developing strong self-knowledge and ensure that what we *feel* matches our tone of voice, body language, and message. The more we can ensure that students keep their dignity when we respond to them during a difficult situation, the more we will see better relationships within the classroom through students' greater self-awareness and self-control.

To what extent do we value students' ideas and leadership? When we care about student initiative, we find ways to support it. Perhaps the most powerful and successful way to build responsibility is to *include* students in all aspects of establishing a classroom that supports learning and personal growth.[2] Student-led classroom meetings can be a powerful process to affirm students' competence and develop their social skills.[3] As well, students benefit greatly from lessons and activities that increase their understanding of the needs and feelings of others.[4] Appendix D is designed to support that task.

It can be easy to forget that our students have lots of social and practical skills and exercise them away from school. Most parents are not afraid of walking out of a room and leaving their children alone. Teenagers often hold jobs and spend time away from constant adult supervision, and usually rise to the trust that is shown to them. Working toward an honor system in your classroom demonstrates trust.

Collaborative activities involve students' hearts as well as their bodies. They also generate a certain type of energy in the classroom where students feel free to express their ideas and where the teacher's calmness, serenity, and imagination support them. If we think about our interactions in schools as fields of energy mingling together, the next step is to consider how we can shift this energy in positive ways. These ways of including students' ideas ensure our own growth as teachers. We become stronger, more trusting, flexible, and caring as our students grow in these same ways. The atmosphere improves through mutual respect and positive regard.

When we come to know our students as persons and they see us demonstrating patience, honesty, hope, and courage, this provides a positive shift and a safety net for students. A safe environment supports students in becoming involved and increases responsibility incrementally while strengthening their capabilities. By developing caring relationships with students and showing an interest in their lives, we create positive energy in the classroom while expanding students' academic knowledge, and their personal and social capabilities. This includes a heightened awareness and use of their emotional intelligence.

Some Questions to Ask Are:

- What personal qualities help me to create positive energy in the classroom?
- What strategies do I use to build relationships with students to increase student voice and leadership?
- How do I demonstrate fairness and respect for all students? Show interest in them as persons?
- How does a negative atmosphere in the classroom affect my spirit and the spirit of my students, in the short term and the long term?
- To what extent is the need to create positive energy in the classroom for our benefit as teachers? To what extent will it contribute to student learning?

Some Practices to Consider Are:

- If a problem occurs in the classroom, internally assess the situation and your own feelings, and determine a responsive approach that supports the students (or yourself) in acting differently. This is particularly important to consider if disruptive interactions keep recurring with individual students. Sometimes you may have to say, "I'm not happy with what's happening and feeling upset right now, let's all take a few moments to calm ourselves, and then I will respond to what just happened." Students will appreciate the authenticity of this admission.

- As part of your planning, reflect on those teacher qualities that support a safe and caring classroom atmosphere, which are strengths of yours, and how you might exemplify them during the school day.
- Dialogue groups: At one of your teacher group sharing sessions, you may want to dedicate time to discussing strategies that strengthen student involvement and responsibility. Expanding your repertoire and that of your colleagues in this regard can be helpful in supporting a productive school environment.

Thoughts to Remember

As teachers we need to have clarity about the vision we have for a healthy classroom environment and the values and personal qualities we bring to it. Honesty, sincerity, warmth, and trustworthiness are qualities that can be cultivated through increasing our awareness of when and how we demonstrate them. Dignity is such a strong word and it is a concept that we need to keep as a touchstone for all our responses to students. Preserving the dignity of an individual student models a respectful response which benefits all class members. It is a powerful model for the behavior of all class members. The challenges of classroom management and unruly student behavior have proved to be the greatest source of teacher stress, so having a touchstone is invaluable.

Students crave for opportunities to contribute to classroom life and we can support that in many ways including seeking their input and supporting student voice. All the ways that you can find to have a stable and warm environment pay dividends in reduced stress and increased enjoyment for you and better learning and increased emotional safety for students.

NOTES

1. See, for example, Elias (2012), Haberman (2004), and Cervini Manvell (2009).
2. To mention but a few of the well-presented arguments for involving students in central classroom decisions, see Amstutz and Mullet (2005), Curwin and Mendler (1999), Kohn (2011), Shapiro and Skinulis (2000), and Wells (1986).
3. Helpful models of class meetings can be found in Glasser (1965), Fitzell (1997), and Amstutz and Mullet (2005).
4. For a wealth of practical classroom ideas related to developing students' knowledge and abilities in their emotional and social dimensions, see *Strong Spirits, Kind Hearts* (Finney, 2013).

Chapter 16

Writing Our Teaching Life

> A well-known writer got collared by a university student who asked, "Do you think I could be a writer?"
> "Well," the writer said, "I don't know.... Do you like sentences?"
> The writer could see the student's amazement. Sentences? Do I like sentences? I am twenty years old and do I like sentences? If he had liked sentences, of course, he could begin, like a joyful painter I knew. I asked him how he came to be a painter. He said, "I liked the smell of paint." (Dillard, 1990, p. 70)

Reasons for writing about your teaching do not have to be any more complicated than liking sentences or the smell of ink, but the rewards of doing so can be many. The ways to do so are equally numerous. Personal writing can reveal aspects of your teaching formerly unnoticed and be a source of discovery. It can be a cache of questions to explore, a memory bank, a conversation with yourself, or an art form. It need not only be a record, the bare bones of what happened on the surface of classroom interactions, nor restricted to your plan for a lesson or a day of lessons. Rather, writing out of a creative center, a playful mind, or from your heart could become a pleasure and form of renewal. This is particularly so if you allow your writing to be idiosyncratic, in your own style, and in your unique voice.

Teaching can be fatiguing – it draws on all our resources and at the end of the day, it is common to feel spent. Out of this tiredness in need of calm, or edginess in need of distraction, might come an insight, a precious nugget that only revealed itself because you are committed to a practice of writing a sentence or two to describe the quality of your day. The trick to this is being able to write spontaneously, quickly, not knowing in advance what you are going to say. Months later reviewing these end-of-day musings, you might discover a truth or a pattern of ideas that can be used to enrich your teaching. Sharing these discoveries with colleagues can also add to the store of their knowledge or give them a new idea to try.

Personal qualities that support our writing practice include curiosity, honesty, imagination, and being a keen observer. These are also the qualities that are strengthened through writing about our school day, our feelings, and new insights. Through writing we learn more about ourselves. It is a versatile tool for both personal and professional growth.

Perhaps you might start your writing practice in a small way rather than commit to doing some writing every day other than that which your job requires, you might simply try to write once a week or when the spirit moves you. You are more likely to keep and enjoy a practice if it doesn't seem a burden. The writer Anne Lamott describes the advice her father gave to her little brother when he was trying to write a report on birds and was feeling overwhelmed.

> He was at the kitchen table close to tears, surrounded by binder paper and pencils and unopened books on birds, immobilized by the hugeness of the task ahead. Then my father sat down beside him, put his arm around my brother's shoulder, and said, "Bird by bird, buddy. Just take it bird by bird." (1994, p. 19)

To avoid writing as if it were a chore, it is important to write something that has a lot of meaning to you, that you have fun writing, or that you know will be useful in the future. You might start writing a list of adjectives that describe your students' personalities or adverbs describing the various ways they tackle learning tasks and respond to your explanations.

One of the challenges of teaching is that of writing comments in report cards. Having lists that describe qualities and behaviors of the students you are teaching can make this task easier and at the same time keep it authentic. Another useful form of writing is to develop a list of all the adjectives and phrases you can think of which describe qualities of the types of assignments you typically have your students complete.

A comment on a math assignment might require different words than that in response to a student's poetry. The more adjectives and adverbs you have at your disposal, the better your responses could become. You can have fun with these lists and include ones that you might never use. However, this type of brainstorming with yourself can increase your awareness of students' personalities and your knowledge of what you are looking for in an assignment and therefore what you want to stress in your teaching.

One of the ideas of writing spontaneously, informally, and in our own voice, is to draw on our sense of playfulness to relieve any stresses of the day. Did we notice an incident that could be considered funny if we didn't feel so responsible for it? Without becoming cynical, we can sometimes use literary devices such as exaggeration to release some of the distress we feel such as at administrative directives that do not appear to be student-centered.

Another form of writing that is valuable is to write in order to express negative emotions, to reflect on the situations that triggered them, and to come to terms with them and let them go. A lot of research confirms this. For example, Pennebaker (1997) and his colleagues have conducted many studies that demonstrate the ways that expressing emotions through writing can promote both mental and physical health.

Whether or not you have had a writing practice in the past, whether or not you teach writing, you can discover your own gifts as a writer. Just as teachers need to read to develop greater depth and imagination in their teaching, they need to write to find their voice, discover personal "ah-ha" moments, and deepen their abilities for reflection and intuition. One suggestion in relation to developing greater insight into your own thoughts and feelings is to imagine that your heart or soul is doing the writing and informing your head.

You don't need to restrict your writing to a focus on your teaching. Writing about any aspect of your life or thoughts can provide you with insights about yourself, your worries, dreams, or struggles with another person. Writing can be an insightful process if you let it take you where it wants to go and you discover, "Oh, I thought I was writing about this, but I was really writing about that" or "I didn't know I thought that!"

Using the personal form of writing for professional growth – allowing it to ramble freely increases the likelihood that you *will* keep a record and that you will enjoy doing so. As you develop a practice of personal writing, your teaching may seem more and more to be an enriching training ground for becoming fully human and fully alive. In a way similar to what you feel about the individuality of each of your students, you may affirm,

> My thoughts are unique, because I am a singular being and these thoughts come from me, they pass through this body, are in this mind and heart, and carry my experiences. Even though others may have similar thoughts, they do not arise in the same source mine do. My writing is unique in this same way because it is *my* voice that is being expressed.

This is a cause for celebrating being alive, being here, and being you, and a reason to write your life and teaching life in your own singular voice.

Some Questions to Ask Are:

- Do I restrict my teaching-related writing to lesson plans and report cards? Do I see ways that my lesson plans and report cards might benefit from adding another writing practice to my teaching life?

- Have I noticed that I remember things better if I write them down? What about my teaching life do I want to remember?
- Can I allow my personal writing to be messy and imperfect, non-grammatical, or incomplete? Do I have a tendency for perfectionism that might stifle my ability to write freely, off the top of my head and without editing my thoughts?
- Am I able to sit down and start writing about anything that comes to mind and be comfortable shifting direction as the writing progresses?
- Are there ways we could support each other to undertake more personal writing within our lives as teachers? Could our dialogue group or staff meeting include a few minutes of personal writing in relation to professional concerns and school experiences? How might this enrich the discussions which follow?

Some Practices to Consider Are:

- A practice that may come to be pleasurable is to write one sentence at the end of each day that captures a moment where real learning happened, when you saw a light go on in several faces. The more you use this practice, the more you will become aware of them and work to increase them. When you read these one-sentence histories of your teaching at the end of each month or year, you could feel rewarded that you wrote them and grateful that you chose to be a teacher.
- When you are worrying about something that happened in your teaching or puzzling over how to reach a difficult student or please a demanding principal, write a description of it and how you feel. In doing this type of writing, you may find out more about what you think and how you feel.
- Dialogue groups: With the teacher friends or colleagues with whom you meet regularly, brainstorm a list of all the ways students' individuality could be described. On another occasion, you might focus this free-flowing group thinking on ways to describe the qualities found in students' completed assignments. Alternatively, each time you gather you might include a practice of writing a short response to an important topic or concern as a way to deepen the conversations you have together.

Thoughts to Remember

When using the personal form in writing about your teaching life, the first principle to remember is to write for enjoyment. The second and third are to let go of standards of what length it should be and to make your writing a self-criticism-free zone. Spontaneity can reveal insights we didn't realize we held.

There are many possibilities for recording your life in the classroom from descriptions of your feelings, a remarkable student insight, to analyses of lessons or surprising things that happened. You can use them all and write a word or two during the teaching day, a few sentences at the end of the day, or a longer piece whenever it seems to flow from your fingertips. Personal writing can improve your morale and the quality of your teaching and generally enrich your life.

Part III

TO ENRICH AND DEEPEN OUR BEING

Make time for soulfulness within your own life. Allow yourself time for self-renewal, be it walking in the woods, sitting quietly, listening to music, praying, meditating, or sharing time with people you love. Fill your own heart with gratitude, joy, and peace, and your contentment will naturally radiate to others.[1]

NOTE

1. Dalton, J. & Fairchild, L. (2004). *The Compassionate Classroom: Lessons that Nurture Wisdom and Empathy*, p. x.

Chapter 17

Opening the Mind

> If we think about it, life resists definition. How can we truly know things that constantly change, are impossible to pin down, and are always open to interpretation? Can we, for instance, ever reach absolute conclusions about the redness of a flower, a moment of grief, or the meaning of the universe? (Mattis-Namgyel, 2010, p. 13)

We all have a sense that we know many things and the stable things of our world – our table, our dishes, the sun coming up in the morning, and the switch turning the light off *are* knowable. There are other aspects of our life, as Mattis-Namgyel reminds us, that are ultimately unknowable but enriching to ponder. We have so many possibilities for opening the mind, freeing ourselves from prejudices and narrowness, and many rewards for doing so. There is nothing so freeing to the spirit as the gifts of an open mind.

An open-minded teacher is also more likely to be fair, collaborative, interested in other viewpoints, curious, and adaptable. We are more able to value and personify these qualities when we know the moral limits of our openness. We are clear that we oppose the destructiveness of violence, abuse, racism, and other damaging cultural and ethnic prejudices. Instead we ground our openness in kindness, respect, and touchstones like the golden rule.

The open mind is an explorer. Not attached tightly to views, it is free to roam and discover new ways to see the world. When we achieve this quality of the mind, even for a few minutes, our creativity is awakened, life's possibilities expand, and we are more alive. The opposite of the open mind is a sense that we can know and control our life from moment to moment.

With this need for control, we may have done the planning of lessons and tests, pegged all our students as smart or not so smart, and as well behaved or potential troublemakers and acted accordingly throughout the day, based on this sense of knowing what's what. We have just tightened our world, our mind, and ultimately our heart. In this way of being, there is no room to respond to an important world event, a student who has lost a loved one, an administrative interruption, or a comedic moment. All are buried under "the plan" for the curriculum, the pegging of students, and our fixed idea of who we are as a teacher and a person.

We can release some of the tension that develops when we are operating in control mode by remembering that others are also our teachers. Notice how openness increases your spontaneity and helps you discover more "teachable moments." These moments arise as a form of letting go and often start by really listening to our students and being willing to go where their ideas are taking everyone's thinking. Teachable moments come from being fully present, which is one quality of an open mind.

Openness allows us to see possibilities even within challenges and every day becomes a new day with its puzzles and rewards. Starting each day afresh means we are prepared to learn from and be surprised by our students. We can be more attentive to their individual needs by not having too many preconceived notions about them or limits on ways that they can be themselves and participate with us. We forgive yesterday's misbehaviors, and perceive the ways that our students are changing, learning, and growing. When we are open in these ways, we strengthen our relationship to them.

Openness often requires that we have the ability to remain unthreatened by a possible challenge that someone or something presents to our particular perspective. Such challenges tend to raise our assumptions for examination, thereby revealing any prejudices we may have. For Gadamer (1999), openness requires that we bring these prejudices into play and recognize "that I myself must accept some things that are against me, even though no one else forces me to do so" (p. 361).

This means that we are willing to consider that others (including texts) may have something worthwhile to say to us, and that we are able to open ourselves to truly trying to understand what that is. By thinking about and trying to strengthen the others' viewpoint or position, we come to understand it more fully and may be surprised by what we discover.[1] New possibilities of understanding arise when we are surprised or confronted by information that does not align with our current understanding. Perhaps we could start to welcome these as gifts that might open us to more of life.

There are other benefits of becoming more aware and able to approach each moment with curiosity. Approaching our teaching with openness supports students to ask "Why?" and "What if?" and you to ask, "What do *you* think?" When we model a respect for uncertainty and the place of doubt in research and scholarship, we help to lessen prejudice and increase the emotional safety of classroom discussions.

An open mind can also lead us to a more open heart – one willing to be touched by awe and love for delicate things, as well as grand ideas and wild storms. Perhaps one of the most precious gifts of opening our minds is the capacity to wonder.

> *In my childhood, I learned that bugs were a problem to be avoided. My mother was afraid of bees and wasps, felt mosquitoes and flies existed to be swatted, and found earthworms abhorrent so I did too. That changed when I was a kindergarten teacher. I wanted my students to appreciate all the diverse life forms in their world.*
>
> *I developed a series of lessons about insects and together we were astonished to find all the different kinds of ladybugs in the neighbourhood. We found yellow ones and red ones and counted the different numbers of spots they had. I also learned how open my students were to such discoveries and their interest and excitement was contagious. I was inspired by it.*
>
> *Not long after this focus on ladybugs, one of my students came into the classroom with a big smile and an air of excitement. He was so happy when he told me I was going to be really surprised to see what he brought for sharing time that I didn't want to dampen his enthusiasm in any way. When we were all seated on the carpet in our circle, I suggested he go first. He emptied his pockets onto the rug and a mound of soil crawling with earthworms appeared before us.*
>
> *I felt clear I wanted to show I was pleased with this show of enterprise and said something like, "Wow!" From the other children came the "oohs!" and "ughs!" then the flurry of questions like "How do they move? Where are their feet?" These creatures too became interesting and we talked about why they were good for gardens. I think the loss of prejudice against some life forms marked a significant shift in my ability to be as curious as my students.*

It can be life-enriching when we ask "What is this?" or "What am I seeing? What am I hearing?" These questions can be asked about a dandelion or a Bach partita. Such questions come from a sense that there is more to know about simple things or deeper pleasures. The main purpose of asking these questions is to open yourself to larger possibilities, to spark your creativity, and to lessen your prejudices or preconceived notions about yourself and your world.

When we are no longer curious about life's mysteries and not questioning, our world narrows. We may feel safer and content with what we know of reality. At the same time, we may miss some of the gifts that life offers the curious, wondering, and open mind.

> Everyday life is wondrous. . . . Children see this miracle in a blade of grass. How many blades are there in the world? They experience it when they encounter by surprise a friend from their old neighbourhood. It's miraculous when the training wheels come off their bikes. And who can forget the magic of the letters of the alphabet becoming words that you can read! (McCarty, 2006, p. 67)

Each day offers us new possibilities for finding meaning. For a moment, the sun hits a dandelion and it glows with beauty; a bird sings just when our heart needs uplifting; we see our loved one anew and we are refreshed. There is more to learn, and more questions to ask about what is most important and worthwhile. To live our lives as a response to a world that contains mystery as well as majesty, uncertainty, unpredictability, constant change, and suffering as well as joy, we need to keep our most important questions alive.

It can be as freeing not to know as it is confining to want to always be in control and trying to protect our beliefs and behaviors from any possibility for change. It would enrich our lives greatly if we could embrace more of our experiences with a child's sense of awe and wonder, and approach life with an openness that includes gentleness and respect.

Some Questions to Ask Are:

- Do I know the limits to my openness? What behaviors do I not tolerate? What experiences shut me down? How easy or difficult is it for me to avoid creating stereotypes of people who are quite different from me culturally or in their looks, behaviors, and mannerisms? Do I form hasty opinions about the likely values and life styles of, for example, someone riding a motorcycle, a politician, or a salesperson?
- What are some of the big-picture questions I ponder? What do I wonder about but can't ever know?
- When confronted with seemingly conflicting views, do I use the concept of "both/and" rather than "either/or" to keep my thinking open? That is, do I consider the possibility that both of these views may be true in some way or in some context and that there may be more possible views that I haven't thought of yet? What helps me to do this?
- What physical, emotional, aesthetic, and spiritual needs do I have?[2] In what ways do these needs, if unmet, prevent me from being open?
- Do we have ways to support students to wonder about questions of meaning and purpose?

Some Practices to Consider Are:

- Periodically, take the time to reflect on the ways that everything changes – sometimes suddenly, sometimes slowly. Even rocks are gradually worn away. Knowing that we can't know the changes the next moment holds is a good way to remain open to wider possibilities.
- Take "Be open" as your motto for a week. An open mind is more attentive to the present and aware of its surroundings. Notice how openness increases your spontaneity and helps you to notice more "teachable

moments." This ability to be attentive without an agenda starts with really listening to students and being able to let go of your plan or preconceived notions of what they want to learn.
- Dialogue groups: Within your teacher network, discuss the importance of questions and reflections related to purpose and meaning. Explore ways to support students to ask more big questions – ones that really matter to them.[3]

Thoughts to Remember

Life has mystery as well as majesty, patterns and stability, chaos and beauty. The glory of appreciating that many things are beyond our control is the sense of freedom we feel, and the curiosity and childlike wonder we retain. The open mind learns more, feels more, and lives more fully. It is helpful to reflect on what might be preventing us from being open by exploring our intellectual, social, emotional, and spiritual needs. Unmet needs such as for emotional safety can prevent us from experiencing the gifts of an open mind.

Our students benefit greatly from our openness to them and their ideas, questions, and needs. We can be their role model for letting go of prejudices, considering ideas that don't agree with our own, and accepting, even enjoying, the uncertainty that is part of being alive.

NOTES

1. See Thurgood Sagal (2009) for further description regarding this practice related to Gadamer's philosophical hermeneutics (pp. 17–18).
2. According to Rosenberg (2012), basic needs we all have include the need for: autonomy, celebration, integrity, interdependence, physical nurturance, play, and spiritual communion.
3. See Finney (2013), Chapter 7.

Chapter 18

Nurturing Our Love of Learning

> The word *philosophy* means "love of wisdom." Inspired by a sense of wonder and countless questions, philosophers investigate life. Ordinary things usually taken for granted acquire a new meaning when we look deeper and ask ourselves, "What's going on?" The more often such a seemingly simple question is asked, the bigger the world appears and the more curious the questioner becomes about that world. Regardless of age, *anyone* who sets out to explore the unexplained, to ponder the mysterious is by definition a philosopher. (McCarty, 2006, pp. 1–2)

This curiosity about the world and need to explore it is intensely striking with babies and toddlers who make amazing progress each day, as they interact with their surroundings in novel ways. When they fail to roll over, reach the mobile, or stand up unaided, young children continue to push themselves through difficult trials and multiple attempts. Similarly, when learning to ride a two-wheeled bicycle as children, we experience many falls and scrapes. Yet, we continue to try as our spirit remains undaunted in relation to fulfilling our need to learn to ride a "grown-up" bike.

Young children are tireless when it comes to pushing the boundaries of learning. As we continue to develop through the school years and beyond, some of us appear to demonstrate a stronger inner growth need than others. For others, unfulfilled emotional needs may get in the way of learning. Yet, we are all born with an innate drive to explore the limits of our physical, social, intellectual, and spiritual dimensions to varying degrees. The profession of teaching is one that calls us to be lovers of wisdom, to love learning new things, to more deeply understand old ideas we hold, and to ignite this spark of curiosity and wonder in our students. Our students are philosophers of life and through our own love of learning we can inspire them to continue to question and persevere with discovery and creation of new learning and to attain new abilities.

Learning to ride a two-wheeled bicycle or drive a car is usually something we do because we want to. In other situations, we begin to learn about a topic or potential area of interest because we are required to. Many post-secondary programs require their students to explore areas outside of their major field of study. This required exploration may lead to increased interest when the teacher's own love of learning supports students to get into a topic more deeply. For example, enrolling in an introductory geology class can lead to class outings to study rocks while enrolling in an introductory drama class can culminate in a school drama production.

Cervini Manvell (2009) affirms that successful teachers are lifelong learners. This entails being open to deep internal needs that draw our attention to exploratory options and being willing to take the risks that such learning entails. What if we are not successful? What if we find out that our current practice is flawed? What if we discover our new practice works better to support our students' learning? These types of questions let us know that we are approaching the edge of our expertise and that we are willing to take the risk to work beyond this edge.

Larrivee (2012) believes that lifelong learning "promotes risk taking, inventing, and exploring" (p. 11). When we are willing to take a risk, we find that our explorations are more open and that our curious, creative, inventive selves can come forward. Finney (2013) recognizes the wisdom of keeping our feelings of wonder alive. Wondering about ourselves, others, and our environment has the potential to fuel our creative drive and urge for transcending our limitations, which, in turn, nourish our spiritual development. One of the rewards of teaching is following our interest in learning about the mysteries of the world and sharing this passion for learning with our students.

Passion is catching and lights a learning environment with fire and enthusiasm. Students not only see but they can sense when we are captured by an idea, event, or process. They are drawn into the questioning, wondering phase and are keen to join us on this exciting, learning journey. Inventing and exploring are contagious and affect ourselves and our students at a very deep level. We are never the same after experiencing learning of this nature. We can never quite go back to viewing the world or learning about it in the same way we did before we engaged in this learning experience together.

When I got my first teaching job, I was teaching middle years students. I took advantage of every workshop given by practising teachers to learn about different teaching methods. When I returned from a cooperative learning workshop, I tried think-pair-share, four-square, jigsaw, and other cooperative learning methods with my grade nine students.

> They enjoyed the interactive nature of these methods along with the opportunity to learn with and about their fellow students. Our classroom and our learning activities were never the same after these experiences. Even when I didn't explicitly build in cooperative learning processes, my students found ways to spontaneously collaborate every day. This pushed me to learn about more open, interactive ways to design my lessons.

One of the lovely aspects regarding the journey of teaching is that, in a sense, there is no final destination or endpoint – we will never arrive. We will never learn all there is to learn about the science and art of teaching. We will never reach the endpoint of deepening our practice through engaging with our students and varied learning experiences. We will always have new challenges we want to explore and, therefore, new ideas we want to learn about. We will always have a new group of students and, subsequently, new strategies that we want to incorporate into our classroom practice to facilitate optimal student learning. Teaching is a profession that pushes us to think deeply, to care about others, to model morally strong behavior, to draw on our imagination, to take risks, and to continue to learn.

Teaching is a humanitarian and scholarly career. When we nurture our love of learning, we nurture the compassionate and scholarly part of ourselves. Not all jobs or careers offer so many opportunities for continued learning and growth, or what some might describe as challenges that require us to build our skill level or rethink our professional goals. Lifelong learning is a way to engage in scholarly pursuits which can arise from opportunities, challenges, or inner growth needs. In some cases, it is difficult to put one's finger on why one feels drawn to engage in a particular activity.

> When I was a high school student, I enjoyed French language classes and chose to study French at university. I obtained my teaching degree with a major in French. Over my teaching career, I taught all grade levels but ended up teaching in multi-grade situations in rural communities which placed my interest in the French language on a back burner.
>
> In my last decade of work, I engaged in curriculum development with the provincial Ministry of Education. At that point, I was in a large city which offered French language courses in the evenings and on weekends. I decided to enrol in these extension courses and when friends asked me if this would give me a higher salary at work, I told them "no." Then they asked if learning French would give me a promotion at work. Again, my response was "no." I finally explained my interest by acknowledging that this was a deep interest that I had – a need – and that I was engaged in a process of learning for the love of learning – an end in itself.

Lantieri (2001) notes the importance of teachers "engaged in inquiry, exploring and learning about what has heart and meaning for themselves"

(p. 8). Nurturing our love of learning is a powerful practice and allows us to experience the rewards of efforts that push us beyond where we thought we might reach. In all cases, learning allows us to explore aspects of ourselves and the world from different perspectives. It also contributes to who we are as a person in the universe.

As in the personal teacher story above, we may not have a practical reason for why we engage in a particular learning experience. In some situations, we take advantage of opportunities that present themselves. In other situations, we have a challenge that we want to address. In yet other situations, we have a strong inner growth need that we choose to follow. While the challenge is the immediate impetus for engaging in learning, this motive may shift as we participate in the learning experience to one of learning simply for the pleasure of learning. Following our heart will help us make critical decisions as lifelong learners and will enrich our learning, our teaching, and our spirit.

Some Questions to Ask Are:

- What am I curious about? What do I want to explore? When have I been compelled to learn? In what ways has this learning enriched my being?
- How am I learning, changing, and growing as a result of my teaching? How does this fulfill an inner growth need of mine?
- What new learning have I engaged in over the last five years? What impelled me to take on this new learning? What aspects of my classroom practice and my spirit have been nourished by this learning?
- How do I engage with the curiosity and wonder of my students and encourage them to follow their interests and learn for the pleasure of learning?
- What are we thinking about and working on in relation to our teaching journey or the learning challenges in our school? What new learning might this require? What aspects of ourselves and our teaching lives will this new learning enrich?

Some Practices to Consider Are:

- Consider an aspect of your classroom practice to explore to discover what has "heart and meaning" for you. Choose something that you are being nudged to learn about, then design a potential inquiry. Refer to Appendix C for a sample plan related to "Observing my Own Teaching."
- Foster your own and your students' curiosity and learning. Follow up on interests, questions, and experiences as a catalyst for creating communities of curiosity and learning. Think about how curiosity and the related learning energize your classroom.

- Dialogue groups: Suggest that your teacher network or staff focus for a month on taking some risks in trying new things or learning just for the sake of learning. Make the emphasis of this learning on something that would strengthen student learning, expand your teaching repertoire, and feed the soul.

Thoughts to Remember

Not all career choices offer the lifelong learning possibilities that teaching does. This is a blessing of the teaching profession that stems from our openness to explore ideas with our students, our interest in their questions, and the energy that comes from our sense of wonder. A gift that we bring to our students and colleagues is the gift of our curiosity and passion to know something deeply – finding the hidden meanings in content we are required to teach. When we understand that learning new skills and ideas is energizing and satisfying, even exhilarating, we are motivated to seek out the next learning adventure.

Learning can be catching as your enthusiasm feeds that of your students. What a rich life and what a boon to our students and ourselves this can be when we continue to act on our desire for new learning and professional and personal growth!

Chapter 19

Discovering the Beauty that Makes Us Whole

Speechless before
These budding green spring leaves
In blazing sunlight.

—Bashō

The seventeenth-century Japanese poet, Matsuo Bashō, understood the human need for beauty and felt one way it could be found was to return to the elemental world of our natural and spiritual origins. This poem was written when Bashō was on a spiritual journey to visit a hermitage and temple high in the mountains. He wrote in the journal he kept on that journey that often the greater the beauty, the less the words can say. He used haiku as a way to express a response to the experience of beauty while keeping it fresh and whole.

Beauty is one of the great needs of the soul. Beauty draws us in and creates a relationship of awe and respect. Beauty inspires, warms, and enlarges us. A quality of the beautiful is also that it is natural in some way. From earliest times, the beautiful has been associated with the good and the true as entwined virtues that enrich our being – each being a necessary component of the other. In a study of the role and nature of aesthetic experiences in daily life (Schaefer, 1996), one participant discussed beauty in a way congruent with this association of the beautiful with the good. He characterized beauty as, "what a person does to try to make their world and the world better . . . to try to make their life in some way meaningful in this difficult world" (p. 63).

In *The Way of Beauty,* François Cheng (2009) suggests that the beautiful is connected to the sacred; it opens us and helps us partake of the infinite within the finite moments of its being seen or heard and felt by the soul. This sense of the infinite he describes as the recognition that all that is beautiful comes from the continuous unfolding and creating of the universe (just as we do). The beautiful calls for protection, causes us to tread more lightly, to be more respectful. This is its relationship to goodness. When we experience beauty as something natural, as deeply genuine, it calls us to gratitude. These are ideas with a far reach and worth pondering but not ones that we necessarily associate with the concept of beauty.

Perhaps our conception of beauty comes most from the way we experience it in everyday life. These experiences are pleasurable for their aesthetic qualities and nourishing for the way they make life seem to have a deeper meaning – one that is enriching. Another way to describe such experiences is to say that beauty draws us into relationship with what we see or hear, and feel. That which is beautiful becomes part of us in a way that can't be bought and sold.

While recognizing that cultural stereotypes related to beauty exist and are not always healthy and life-affirming, we can reject those that make us feel inadequate or imperfect. The recognition of a deeper essence in objects, people, and experiences can lead us to more meaningful ideas of the beautiful and protect us from harmful stereotypes. That which is beautiful can take us out of our smaller selves, strengthen our sense of connection with all living things, and support us in understanding ourselves as a unique and necessary part of the web of life.

Beauty that is open to all of us, regardless of income, comes from many sources that are mostly free and accessible. Seeking such forms of beauty is a practice that involves deepening and expanding our awareness. We can experience forms of beauty in everyday life through noticing, feeling, and appreciating:

- The changing sky
- The ways light illuminates a room, increasing the glow and vibrancy of everyday objects
- The patterns and delicacy in feathers, shells, and other natural objects
- The magnificence of a storm
- The faces and postures of children and others when their whole being is absorbed in what they are doing
- Acts of human compassion, generosity, or love
- The serenity in the faces of some people, particularly in the very old
- The pleasing form of some crafted objects
- The ease, power, and strength of animals when they leap or run
- Bird song, human song, and other music that unites mind and heart.

When we make a practice of sharing some of our encounters with beauty with our students, we are enlarging their own potential to find beauty in daily life. This is a gift that can continue to enrich their life into adulthood. Teachers can educate their students' aesthetic sensibilities in ways that draw all students into conversations and activities by making attention to aesthetics a regular part of classroom life.

In our focus on beauty as teachers, we want to acknowledge that it can be misused in ways that damage spirits such as the stereotypes of female beauty that put pressure on women to maintain unhealthy thinness. To the greatest extent possible, we want our students to experience the beauty of real things both in nature and in art; and to notice the differences between living things and the ways they are depicted. For example, drawing students' attention to the subtlety of color in the natural world or the slight variations in a bird's song educates their perceptual abilities.

> *My teaching career was deeply touched by a visit from a pair of British teachers who showed us slides of their classroom displays. They made a lot of use of fabrics as backdrops, draping them over blocks and boxes to create levels on which were placed a vase of flowers, a piece of pottery, a rock, or a shell. The displays had a simplicity about them, but it was clear that a lot of attention was given to the details. The colours were subtle and often related to the natural world. I took real pleasure in adopting these practices in my classroom.*
>
> *As my aesthetic sensibilities deepened, my ability to appreciate students' creativity and aesthetic sensitivity also increased. One of the most impressive paintings I saw as a teacher came from a grade one boy who painted a hockey player, a goalie so large his body wasn't contained in the painting and his use of colour was bold, simple, and restricted to a few colours. The painting powerfully expressed that no puck was going to get by this goalie.*

We can educate aesthetic sensibilities by encouraging our students to bring things they find in nature such as a stone or a feather into the classroom. This would be an opportunity to remind them that honoring the sacredness and beauty of nature means not damaging the trees, shrubs, or other life forms they see and to not take more than one thing they find beautiful from its place. These objects from nature can become the center of a dialogue that seeks to describe all the colors they see in one small stone or attune themselves to the intricacy of a feather by carefully trying to count each fine part of its whole.

Using art, photography, film, and websites, we can help students to see that cultures have differing conceptions of what is beautiful and also hold many ideas about beauty in common. Older students can discuss the qualities they hear in popular music and attempt to compare these to those in classical music. Clothing styles are another focus for increasing students' awareness of the beauty that lasts and enriches life in contrast to that which creates competitiveness and demeans relationships.

Every day offers opportunities to experience moments of beauty. When we recognize what it is that we find beautiful – whether it be our students' faces when they are fully absorbed, a certain type of music, or backlit trees, we can build these experiences into our day. We can also enlarge our concept of the beautiful in life by opening ourselves and our students to the possibility that the essence of beauty is that it is attached to the good and the true – to reality, genuineness, grace, and a sensitivity that touches the soul.

Some Questions to Ask Are:

- What do I consider to be unhealthy or harmful forms of beauty? How do these ideas of what is beautiful develop? How are they spread?
- What qualities of beauty are admired by different cultures? How do these qualities touch my spirit and relate to my role as a teacher?
- In what ways can I express my own sense of the beautiful in my classroom and my home?
- Do I seek and find beauty in common things and everyday experiences? How does this affect my soul and my teaching?
- Do we talk with each other and our students about what we find to be beautiful and whether these ideas could be incorporated into the school and its surroundings?

Some Practices to Consider Are:

- Reflect on what you find to be beautiful. Try to understand what your prejudices might be in relation to beauty and seek ways to approach the category of the beautiful with a more open mind.
- Look with eyes that seek beauty in your surroundings. You will see beauty when you practice looking for it. Notice how this practice affects your spirit.
- Dialogue groups: See if there are ways to incorporate a focus on beauty into a meeting of your teacher network, book club, or staff. The perspectives of others might open all participants to a larger sense of what beauty could be and its importance in nurturing spirits. Explore ways to improve the aesthetic qualities of the school and to involve students as central participants in this task.

Thoughts to Remember

Rather than diminish us, beauty enlarges us and connects us more fully to our experience of the moments unfolding. Beauty is healing and enlivening and, like everything else in our world, is part of the earth and natural in some way.

We see beauty when we seek it out in nature, in art forms, in people's courageous and compassionate acts, and in everyday objects. We enrich our teaching life and our students' lives by including beautiful natural objects and art forms and ideas of the beautiful into classroom aesthetics and discussions.

Chapter 20

Bringing Forth Our Creativity

> The creative process is a spiritual path. This adventure is about us, about the deep self, the composer in all of us, about originality, meaning not that which is all new, but that which is fully and originally ourselves. (Nachmanovitch, 1990, p. 13)

A theme in the work of Nachmanovitch, Richards (1989), and others who work with and write about the creative process is that it involves finding the heart's voice. This may not be the way that you usually think about creativity. You may be like many people who think that creativity is the province of artists and not feel that you are creative. Yet we all share the creative nature of the universe. Understanding that human creativity has its source in the universe can be the encouragement needed to explore and exercise your own creative inheritance.

Through observing the creativity of the natural world and the glories of the galaxies and knowing we are part of it, our own creative nature is enriched and confirmed. Ecologist and philosopher, Stan Rowe (2006) describes this insight into the source of creativity in this way:

> The universe is creative. In the fifteen billion years since the Big Bang it has evoked cycles of star making, constellations, solar systems, planets, ecosystems, organisms, and humans possessed with a conscious spark of that creativity. (p. 54)

At the same time, it is helpful to observe and remember the ways that everything changes. Trees live, die, and slowly return to the soil as compost. Stars form and also implode and explode. This understanding could also free us to let go of what isn't working, to shift gears, and take new routes to the same destination or to a new one.

When we enlarge our concept of creativity, we enlarge our sense of ourselves and our abilities, and our understanding of others and the world, thus, strengthening our teaching. There is a freshness to responding creatively to classroom encounters that enlivens us, our work, and our students. Teaching then becomes more deeply meaningful and, as psychotherapist and creativity coach Eric Maisel (2002) reminds us, finding meaning in our lives is what we all seek. Engaging life with creativity is a way to enjoy our ingenuity and resourcefulness; to spark our enthusiasm, curiosity; and feel the nourishment our soul seeks.

Barron and Barron in their book *The Creativity Cure* (2012) make a strong case, based on their years of experience, that every person's creative capacity can be increased and that our happiness is linked in many ways to the degree of creativity we experience in our daily life. Everyone has creative gifts to draw upon and life provides boundless opportunities to do so. Conversations are creations. Teaching well, knowing how to spark student interest, support inquiry, or respond to a disruption, all engage us in a creative process.

We see this most clearly when we understand that creativity stems from the heart as much as the head and from the sense of being connected with everything in our environment. The heart feels its way into new perspectives. The bonds we form with our students offer us ways to express this feeling of connection – in a way, our creativity is drawn out of us through the quality of our relationships.

We do not need particular or special artistic gifts to respond creatively to classroom life. We need to care about the spirits of our students and our own spirit, and this caring will be the fuel that fires our inventiveness and keeps the learning alive. Surprise is a gift we can bring to a lesson or to a response. We need to be consistent in our respect for our students yet unpredictable in the ways we begin a class, illustrate an example, or sum up a lesson.

Creativity comes from a trust in ourselves and our intention to do our best, and our ability to accept that things won't always go as planned. The creative processes in daily life are integrative processes – inclusive, non-judgmental, and open. To deepen and broaden our creativity, we need to open to the context we are in, open to possibility, open to our students as more than what we see when we view them through an academic lens. Through this openness, we come to understand that we carry the light of creativity within us. So do our students.

One way that you can honor the importance of creative pursuits and aesthetic sensibilities is to prepare the classroom environment for your students' souls and creative natures. Even as a teacher who moves from classroom to classroom and shares these rooms with other teachers, you can establish a practice of bringing something with you regularly that demonstrates the creativity of nature, of others, or speaks to your own sense of the surprising or the unique. An example of this practice would be putting a painting or photograph on the door they enter one day, and a cartoon or inspiring quotation on another. Once the preparation of the environment is established in students' thoughts as an important aspect of school life, you can invite them to contribute to it.

To enjoy the gifts of creativity, we make use of more than the conscious self – the self that is always focused on specific purposes and outcomes. This means becoming more aware of intuitions, dreams, perceptions, and feelings. It can also mean using all our senses more intently – allowing ourselves to become beguiled by variety, detail, and the unusual. Nature is a rich place to develop these aesthetic sensibilities. We see new forms, sense rhythms, and respond to changing light. We experience the energy, cycles, relationships and patterns in nature of seasons, spirals, branches, and symmetry. We find these energy shifts, rhythms, forms, and repetitions in ourselves and can use them in our teaching and our life.

One of the gifts of human and organic creativity is diversity. Rather than fearing or negatively judging differences in cultures and individuals' looks, mannerisms and constructive ideas, we can celebrate them as making the world a more interesting place. Exploring the diversity of the natural world – what the Chinese referred to as "The 10,000 Things" – can become a lifetime entertainment. When we increase our awareness and appreciation of the diversity that surrounds us, we may better appreciate and express our own uniqueness and free ourselves to be more open, spontaneous, and natural. This in turn supports our students to express more fully their gifts, insights, and questions.

In supporting students to come to these same understandings of diversity and change, and reminding ourselves of our creative place in the universe, we can offer the affirmation that everyone and everything is part of this creativity and that we can create not only ideas, projects, and art works but also our lives.

Some Questions to Ask Are:

- Can I understand myself as a part of each context I am in and connected in some way to everything else in it? Do I see ways to use this understanding and the feeling of connectedness to support my creative endeavors including in my teaching?
- How do I use my creativity at school and at home?
- Am I aware of times in the day or the year/semester when my creative self emerges spontaneously? Is this rhythm reflected by my students?
- How do my reflections and dreams influence my creativity?

- In what ways do we express our creativity in our teaching lives? What fosters creativity in us, in our classrooms, and in meetings? What stifles it?

Some Practices to Consider Are:

- Increase your awareness of human diversity and creativity through making a commitment to notice examples of diverse ideas, artworks, rituals, clothing, speech, and humor, as expressed in the daily news or the people you see throughout your day.
- Draw on your imagination and think with your heart to design questions and activities that might spark your students' reflecting, wondering, imagining, and creating and enrich your teaching life.
- Dialogue groups: Focus a discussion with your colleagues on the idea that the universe is always creating and changing, and that because we are all part of the universe, we all carry creativity within us. Explore ideas about how we can express our creativity through our teaching and encourage it in our students.

Thoughts to Remember

The universe of which you are a part is infinitely creative. That same creativity is part of you and all humans. Let this become a deep understanding that inspires and supports your creativity. You can help your students to develop this same understanding by creating an environment that incorporates natural objects and cultural artifacts that reflect the boundless diversity of the natural and constructed worlds and by valuing your students as unique expressions of life.

When we think of creativity as the "heart's voice" and expand our concept of creativity as a gift we all have, we enlarge our sense of ourselves and our abilities. The classroom atmosphere contains more oxygen and freshness as a result of our pleasure in teaching creatively. It also supports us and our students to be all of who we are – our interesting, unique, creative selves.

Chapter 21

Finding Flow

At first Lee tries to hold his horse back, but then he lets him go. The horse, with some memory of the wild in his genes, instinctively runs with the herd, not toward a particular place, but away, running from something without knowing what it is, wanting to take his cue from horses rather than the man on his back.

(From *Cool Water* © 2010 by Dianne Warren. Published by HarperCollins Publishers Ltd. All rights reserved, p. 243)[1]

Have you ever been engaged in a task only to look up and discover that time has flown by? This engagement is often described as "flow" – that locked-in feeling when we're at our most productive. Visual artists, musicians, writers, scientists, athletes, and others find themselves in a state of flow when engaged in and excelling at their respective activities. Their activity is fluid while their attention is locked in. In the classroom, this fluidity occurs when students and their teacher are deeply engaged in high-level, challenging teaching and learning activities that, with effort, are within everyone's reach.

Such engagement comes about in response to tasks where motivation to participate is high, where there is an extended time frame, where immediate feedback is provided, and where participants feel emotionally secure. For example, when participating in drama as a collective creation, teachers and students (in role) experience a sense of deep concentration – a holistic way of being that unites mind, body, and spirit – as they work together to shape the direction of the drama through negotiation and collaboration. As the drama progresses, participants are challenged to respond to each other as they create and express their respective characters through words and actions.

This immediate form of feedback is what moves the drama forward and allows the participants to become caught up in the dramatic events. When we approach this state of flow, everyone around us benefits. The concentration of one feeds the concentration of many. While teachers often set the stage for students to draw on their intuition and let go of self-consciousness, in the example above, the teacher is also deeply engaged. It is the teacher's ability to enter the flow state through drama that supports the students in finding flow.

Flow can be described and understood in many ways, but is not easily captured in precise language. Like many experiences that touch the spirit, it is helpful to have several ways to approach this understanding. Flow is a form of concentration where we are able to lose ourselves in the moment. It is something we fall into and not something that can be forced. It is as though our physical existence, as something separate from the people, equipment, or materials, is temporarily suspended while we are in the flow state.

We become the character that we are expressing in the drama in context. We find that we are one with the motorcycle as we ride through winding terrain. Our arm is merely an extension of the paintbrush as it moves, apparently unaided, completing a painting that is being created right before our eyes. In these situations, our ordinary, everyday routine is superseded and an instinctual way of being is called upon from our center.

Csikszentmihalyi (2004) describes flow as "a state of heightened focus and immersion in activities such as art, play and work." He further suggests that the secret to happiness is finding "pleasure and lasting satisfaction in activities that bring about a state of flow." Experiencing a state similar to flow in our teaching not only brings lasting satisfaction, it supports us to transcend our everyday selves and pursue our chosen profession with greater passion.

As we worked together on solving the math problem, I could sense my students' quiet excitement and intense concentration as different processes were suggested, tried, and rejected. I too got caught up in the process and before I knew it, the bell had rung. During this state of deep engagement, time seemed to stand still – as if it didn't exist.

When we find flow, we experience an increased ability to concentrate, an increased sense of energy, and the ability to be fully engaged in the activity without self-consciousness. In the opening quote, Lee's horse instinctively moves into a flow state when he joins the herd of wild horses and Lee, as the rider, also benefits from this flow state. Lee's horse is mesmerized by the presence of the moving herd and his spirit is awakened. Experiencing flow is rejuvenating for the spirit and, once experienced, may inspire us to create the conditions for it to be achieved within our teaching practice.

Flow entails "a particular way of appreciating, learning from, and working with whatever happens in everyday life" (Hoff, 1982, p. 6). Lee's horse is able to spontaneously draw upon his knowledge of life in the wild that is stored in his genes. We too can experience something of that freedom of acting in accord with our true nature – an adventure that occurs only because we have the confidence and ability to draw on this deep part of ourselves where actions are fluid and spontaneous. This spontaneity is something that emanates from our center and contributes to our feelings of ease and deep engagement.

Larrivee (2012) observes that "successfully managing today's classroom requires a teacher to remain fluid and able to move in many directions, rather than being stuck in automatic responses to situations" (p. 74). Lantieri (2001) also notes the importance of spontaneity or the ability to be flexible and actively adaptive. Spontaneity, fluidity, and flexibility allow us to find reasonable solutions to daily challenges and strengthen our engagement with classroom and school life.

I couldn't believe how the morning class flowed. Students were working on their science experiments in small groups. I was able to highlight the interim results of one group's experiment so that the other groups were able to adjust their processes. When a "rogue" group went off on a tangent using unstable materials, I was able to help them think through how they could take advantage of this "error." I was deeply engrossed and engaged with the students and their partial successes, mishaps, and flops. It was like I had a sense of freedom and spontaneity that I could draw upon on the fly.

The more we experience and discover about our own abilities for using intuition, acting with spontaneity, and responding creatively, the more we see teaching as an opportunity for engagement and discovery.

So, how is it that we can find flow? What does it mean in the classroom? Most of us are familiar with flow as a solitary activity. In the classroom, the overarching condition is an environment where the emphasis is on learning for the love of learning – an atmosphere in which learning is viewed as pleasurable and an end in itself. That is, it is not undertaken simply for marks but to stretch oneself and take pleasure in the process as much or more than the end product. This requires extended periods of time for teachers and students to pursue their goals and receive feedback on how they're progressing. For the flow state to appear in a classroom setting, teachers need to be engaged in the process with their students – exploring interests, following leads, and changing direction.

Participating in a flow state is an active process that requires a high level of skill and competence. If we are learning to do something for the first time, it is unlikely that we will enter a state of flow. After some practice, skill development, and comfort with the process, we are ready for more challenge and deeper engagement. This is when we may find flow. When experiencing the flow state, we are fully engaged in doing something meaningful. We are pulled into the process and open to the unexpected – to discovery.

It is like a deep part of ourselves is called into action and our skill and expertise are drawn upon in challenging ways. We become so completely engaged in the process that we seem to have a clear sense of what to do next. There is no panic or rush but rather a strong sense of serenity as we clearly know what we are doing despite our level of expertise being pushed near its present limit. This causes us to concentrate more fully in order to remain part of the fluid process underway.

When considering how to support the possibilities for flow in the classroom, it might be helpful to think about our knowledge of participating in a sport, playing an instrument, designing a space, or the last time we were deeply engaged in an activity with our students. These reflections may help to raise our awareness of moments where moving into a flow state occurs naturally.

When our senses are heightened and we are keenly aware of our environment, we can more easily see the need to shift or move our attention and subsequent actions in particular ways. This shifting provides an opening through which our spontaneity can flourish. Our engagement and flexibility is nurtured by our feeling for our relationships with others, our materials, and our own wholeness.

Some Questions to Ask Are:

- How can I live more of my life in a fluid, spontaneous state?
- What activities do I engage in where I experience inner clarity and serenity while being deeply focused and challenged?
- When have I experienced time flying by with my students? What activities have we been engaged in?
- How can I bring the spontaneous, effortless feeling of flow more often into classroom activities?
- What might we do when we understand flow but cannot access it? How might we help each other understand how we enter a fluid state as a possibility for enriching our teaching practice?

Some Practices to Consider Are:

- Notice when you are really involved in a process – how everything seems to be going smoothly as you enter a state of flow. For example, when a student asks a question and your response engages the whole class in meaningful questioning and hypothesizing, and before you know it, your lesson has

gone over the time allotted (and you haven't even noticed the time flying by).
- Find space in your day or week where you can allow yourself to enter a fluid relaxed state. For example, go for a bike ride on weekend mornings or sketch in your journal while relaxing on a park bench or at a campsite. Notice if these activities move you into a flow state.
- Dialogue groups: With your colleagues, designate time at one of your networking meetings to talk about the concept of flow and how it influences the practices in your classrooms and the school. Take turns describing experiences where you found flow during an activity with your students. Use this opportunity to enjoy the energy, sense of connection, and feeling of accomplishment that accompanied the experiences.

Thoughts to Remember

Flow can be described as acting in a state of ease and harmony with the materials, people, and other life forms involved in our present actions. It comes from knowing the process, skill, or set of behaviors well and from being comfortable with who we are and confident in our expertise at that moment in time.

With our deep concentration and heightened focus, we find we lose ourselves in the moment and experience our wholeness, drawing on some innate knowledge that flows spontaneously. Our students and others around us feel this meaningful engagement and benefit from the clarity and serenity that accompany these spontaneous moments when we are involved fully, genuinely, and as our natural selves.

NOTE

1. Also published in the United States as *Juliet in August* by Dianne Warren, copyright © 2012 by Dianne Warren. Used by permission of G.P. Putnam's Sons, an imprint of Penguin Publishing Group, a division of Penguin Random House LLC. UK rights granted by the author. Australian and New Zealand rights granted by Allen & Unwin Pty Ltd.

Chapter 22

Having a Hopeful Spirit

> Honest hope comes only as we experience ourselves changing, and are thus able to believe that "the world" can change. (Moore Lappe, 1991, p. xiiii)

There are many ways to understand what is meant by hope and why it is important for your life as a teacher. Hopefulness, as an orientation we try to maintain in our teaching, is more than wishing for something we perceive as good. Rather, hope needs to be acted upon. It can be understood as a marriage of vision, intention, beliefs, and actions. A helpful vision would be one in which you see your teaching as beneficial to the learning and growth of all your students. A major source of hope is your intention to help rather than hurt, and to contribute to the greater good through teaching. Keeping this intention in your mind, heart, and actions gives a steadiness to your moral life and to your teaching.

Because the well-being of your students rests to a large extent in your belief in them as learners, you need to cultivate a conviction that they can all learn, grow, and change. Such a hopeful orientation comes from your belief in yourself as a teacher who can effect change even in discouraging situations of long standing. As well, hopeful people do not feel alone but rather know they have supports in their life and seek out those colleagues, friends, and family members who can offer moral support, practical advice, or a helping hand. Sometimes your supports may take the form of books and other resources, sometimes support comes from remembering past successes or the inspiration you feel hearing the stories of others who have lived through adversity.

People like Vaclav Havel and Nelson Mandela, who maintained their sense of hope through dark hours and tough times without giving up their belief that good work could still be done, have much to offer others in relation to how one enacts hopefulness. Vaclav Havel has emphasized in his writings from prison and his speeches and writings after he regained his freedom that hope grows in strength when it is *acted* upon, not when what is hoped for is achieved. If we only had hope in the best of times, it would not have the worth it has. Havel (1990) says:

> Hope is a state of mind, not of a state of the world. . . . It is an orientation of the spirit, an orientation of the heart; it transcends the world that is immediately experienced, and is anchored somewhere beyond its horizons. . . . Hope, in this deep sense, is not the same as that joy that things are going well, or willingness to invest in enterprises that are obviously heading for success, but rather an ability to work for something, because it is good. (p. 181)

In difficult and potentially discouraging situations in our life, we can avoid despair by turning inward to our spirit as the ultimate source of hopefulness – one stronger than the mind alone. Hope that comes from the spirit is a belief that the actions we engage in must serve the good – that is, the well-being of our students and others. If we feel some practice is harmful to some or all of our students, our hopeful spirit seeks ways to minimize the damage – remembering that, as teachers, we seek to be healers.

A factor that makes a huge difference in how, as teachers, we withstand stress and maintain our health and positive outlook is the extent to which we believe there is always something that we can do to influence a better outcome. This is sometimes called self-efficacy, a belief system that influences how we respond to adversity. The core of this conviction is that rather than being overwhelmed by those aspects of our teaching life that we feel we can't change, we look for some part of them that we can.

We continue to act for the well-being of all our students in whatever ways our imagination and heart can invent. We maintain our belief that there always is something we can do to improve the situation. We do not lose hope in ourselves and we do not lose hope in our students. And we keep thinking until we hit upon the one action or perhaps several actions we can take.

> *I was very grateful for the work of Howard Gardner and others who contributed to the theory of multiple intelligences. This idea that there are many ways to demonstrate and use various forms of intelligence was exactly the kind of theory that I had sensed as a result of my experiences as a teacher but couldn't articulate until I read the research.*
>
> *From that point on, I talked to my students early in the school year with the basic message, "All of you are smart. Even when you consider yourself to be a poor student and think of yourself as "dumb," you are not. We just haven't found the right ways yet to help you learn using the kind of intelligences you have. Some of you are good at sports and have a kind of body intelligence. Some*

of you are kind and know how to make other people feel good. This is another kind of intelligence." I would elaborate on that and make a chart covering all the intelligences that research has described.

I found this to have quite a profound effect on my students, particularly those who were used to struggling at school and felt themselves to be labelled as not very smart (or worse). And in the many discussions that resulted each year from describing the multiple intelligences theory to my students, it was clear they were all aware of and believed the negative labels.

One year, I had a group of grade-five students who all felt they fit the category of poor learners and also considered themselves "bad." As well, many felt they were social outcasts. I talked to them about those feelings and the ways they were wrong. I described the multiple intelligences theory with examples that made sense to them.

One of those students did an unsolicited piece of writing later that day and taped it into the inside cover of his language arts' notebook. (I had asked them to hand them in that day.) This is what he wrote: "I really like scool but I would like school Better if I was smarter than I am know? I think I dum and so does every one iles think I am dum. P.S. Jordan[1] *(original spelling and wording)."*

I phoned and read this to his mother who was reduced to tears. She and her husband started to help Jordan in a couple of subjects in which I thought he had the most potential for growth. I talked to him about what I perceived as his genuine poetic gift giving him some examples, told him how I noticed his kind heart, and he said he was a good hockey player. We talked together about how all of these showed his intelligence.

His father helped him with spelling every night and he beamed when he got his next report card and received the first "B" of his school career. He was used to Ds and Fs. There were so many ways that Jordan was affected by the idea that we all believed in him and could prove to him in real ways that he was a good and intelligent person. He received the gift of hope and this hopefulness fuelled his learning and his happiness.

At the end of the year, I was transferred to a different school and Jordan wrote and illustrated a card for me that I cherish for the sentiment and especially for the way that Jordan intuitively understood and used metaphor. It began, "The world has darkened. The greatest teacher in the world is gone but we will remember her for the big smile she made." Teaching offers us these rare but precious moments when we see how our commitment to our students comes to a positive fruition.

In earlier work, Finney (2013) describes some foundational beliefs about students that are helpful, hopeful, trusting in the potential of all students, and fundamental to good teaching. Central to these beliefs is the conviction that all students are capable of learning and growing.

> Teaching makes no sense without this conviction. You could say, having faith in the abilities of all our students to become more than they reveal at any

given moment is the least we could do. Out of this deeply held belief, we are compelled to give our best. . . . Whether or not you are successful in helping every student believe in themselves, the likelihood of this happening is greatly increased by the steadiness of your faith in their ability to learn. There is a subtle yet powerful difference in atmosphere that pervades a classroom where the teacher sees no student as a failure, every student as potential, and discourages remarks that suggest otherwise. (pp. 5–6)

The conviction that every student can learn and that every child deserves our unfailing support is what makes teaching so rewarding and, at the same time, so challenging. How a teacher acts on their sense of hope is expressed eloquently by Mali (2012):

On a personal level, however, face-to-face with children who have names and stories, who come to school hungry and wearing the same clothes as the day before, you cannot decide that some are no longer worth your time, no matter what the statistics seem to suggest. Teachers who tirelessly fight the good fight know this. No matter how far behind a child is, no matter how limited you think his future choices are, you cannot give up on him. That's what teachers make: the promise to leave every student they teach better prepared for the future than they were when they entered the class at the beginning of the year. On the most basic level, that's just what we do. (p. 193)

Our hopefulness feeds our ability to persevere. When we don't give up on our students or ourselves, we can be at peace with each outcome as it arises – secure in the knowledge that we are doing and giving our best.

Some Questions to Ask Are:

- What are my beliefs about the ability of all my students to learn and grow? Do these beliefs help me when I feel discouraged about a student?
- What inner strengths and which beliefs can I draw upon to continue to be hopeful and to act even when a situation appears to be irretrievable?
- Do I have a vision of the good I intend as a teacher and do I use it to sustain hope and take action in difficult situations?
- How can we transmit our hopefulness to our students and others?

Some Practices to Consider Are:

- Engage with individuals or in activities that sustain or nurture your hopefulness.
- Remind yourself that there is always something that can be done, no matter how small that something might be, and act. Acting for the good has the power to restore your equilibrium.

- Dialogue groups: Make hopefulness a focus for strengthening teaching and undertake the practice of noticing its effects. When reading fiction or nonfiction, and listening to or viewing news and documentaries, notice the role that hope plays in sustaining peoples' spirits and their efforts. Share what you have noticed with your colleagues and discuss ways to enact a hopeful spirit in your teaching.

Thoughts to Remember

A hopeful outlook puts ground beneath your feet – a firm foundation for moving ahead, looking ahead, and seeing possibilities on the horizon. Hope is not wishful thinking but an orientation to a life of doing our best and doing what we can. When close to despair, we turn to our spirit as a constant source of strength. Hope comes from a vision of the good we wish to achieve and from all the small actions we take to bring more goodness into the world.

With hope we don't so much avoid obstacles as chip away at them. This is particularly important in relation to our students. Hopeful teachers believe *all* their students can learn and grow, perhaps becoming discouraged at times but then, trying again to find the way that will help struggling students recognize their progress and increase their belief in themselves. In other words, your hope feeds students' hope that learning is possible and understanding achievable. Then they also try again.

NOTE

1. Jordan is a pseudonym.

Chapter 23

Increasing Happiness in Daily Life

> Humans are creators of meaning, and finding deep meaning in our experiences is not just another name for spirituality but is also the very shape of human happiness. (Rohr, 2011, p. 114)

Happiness can be described as the overall experience of both pleasure and purpose.[1] It is open to everyone despite their particular circumstances, can be increased, and, rather than being a selfish pursuit, our happiness actually contributes to the happiness of others. Happiness is contagious, and when we are happy, those around us feel happier. Happy people are more benevolent and have been described as having a good heart. A happy person has the same ups and downs of every human life, but despite the challenges, even sorrows in their lives, they have an enduring sense of their existence as meaningful. The good news is that we can all learn to be happier and that as teachers, we have a strong sense of purpose and many sources of meaning – they are built in to the teaching life.

In looking at the pleasure dimension of happiness, we can see that it is many faceted from feelings of peacefulness, calm, and contentment to delight, exhilaration, and joy. There are several actions we can take to increase these positive feelings. The first is to become more aware of what makes us happy. We need to make this a conscious focus and really notice our happiness when we are happy.

A good method of increasing this awareness is trial and error, paying attention to the quality of the inner experience. For this to be a powerful practice, it is helpful not to have a vision of happiness that is too rigid or to make too strong a distinction between work and play. Effort, challenge, and struggle can be sources of happiness as we appreciate our perseverance, note our improvements, and just enjoy the process of creating, learning, and working toward something worthwhile. Involvement and deep engagement in the process is often a greater a source of happiness than reaching the goal.

Another way to increase our happiness is to have a gratitude practice. In relation to gratitude, it helps to have a daily practice of asking oneself, "For what in my life am I grateful?" This shifts our thinking from what is wrong with our life to a focus on what is right. Keeping a gratitude journal helps you notice more of the positive aspects of your relationships, work, home, the natural world, and your own attributes. Conversely, gratitude can be undermined by having expectations that are too high or unreasonable.

Authentic feelings of gratitude may be nurtured better by noticing more of the small events and pleasures than the intense ones. A good night's sleep, getting home from work earlier, a short conversation with a colleague that is mutually supportive, a funny observation made by a student or your child can be doubly rewarding – once when experienced and twice, when we recall them and tell them to others or write them down.

One type of happiness that is both pleasurable and health-sustaining is that of experiencing relaxation, calm, and serenity. A key to serenity is to cease comparing ourselves with others – to notice and disengage from feelings of rivalry, inadequacy, or jealousy. Learning to relax includes not only relaxing muscle tension but also allowing our minds to enjoy times of reverie, where our attention can float, frolic, and imagine, where thoughts can flow freely with no particular destination.

Serenity also results from becoming more aware of our thoughts and learning not to identify with them through using practices such as mindfulness and insight meditation. (See Appendix A for an overview of mindfulness.) It is helpful to experiment until we find our own sources of serenity and tranquillity. Our regeneration may come from music, walking, yoga, or coffee with a friend, but what is most important is finding those activities that clear our mind, warm our heart, and bring peace to our soul.

An overarching process that increases happiness is undertaking inner work (i.e., turning inward to better understand our needs, and our thoughts and feelings and their sources). Lenoir (2015) describes the practices of inner work in relation to his own life:

> What has enabled me to be happier through the years is not so much social or material success – even if this has helped – as the *inner* work that has enabled me to improve, to bind the wounds of the past, to transform or move beyond beliefs that made me unhappy, but also to grant myself the right to complete fulfillment in my personal and social life, a right that for a long time I would not give myself [original emphasis]. (p. 53)

He raises an important point here with his last phrase. To be happy we have to believe that we are worthy of happiness. We must feel that we have a right to happiness by virtue of our very existence – of being born with a heart and mind capable of experiencing pleasure and meaning. If we do not accept our inner worth, we tend to ignore or undermine our gifts, accomplishments, and potential, and our capacity for joy.[2] Textbox 23.1 lists a variety of practices of inner work that contribute to greater happiness.

Textbox 23.1 Inner Work that Leads to a Happier Life

1. Believing in our own worth.
2. Granting ourselves the right to be happy.
3. Developing self-compassion.
4. Listening to our heart.
5. Trusting in our ability to overcome problems and integrate sorrows.
6. Know and use our character strengths every day.

We can increase our happiness at school by becoming more aware of our strengths and passions and using these in our teaching and in our relationships with students and colleagues. Passions include such things as cooking, hiking, opera, or a challenging sport. Examples of strengths range from intellectual gifts such as curiosity and open-mindedness to virtues we embody such as fairness and modesty. Three ways to help you learn more about your strengths are to reflect on them yourself, ask others who know you well to describe what they feel your strengths are, and use tests available online such as the ones at www.authentichappiness.org and www.viacharacter.org. Research has shown that making a contribution to the well-being of others through exercising your character strengths and incorporating your passions into your teaching life is gratifying, builds resilience, and can offer you lasting satisfaction.[3]

In relation to the happiness that comes from having a strong sense of meaning and purpose and pursuing life goals, several factors are important to consider. First, research has found that more happiness comes from the journey than from reaching the destination. Working toward a goal gives us more constant and lasting satisfaction than that of actually achieving it and people who have personally significant goals have been found to be happier than those who do not. A second important finding is that the type of goals we set for ourselves matters.

> The goals we set . . . must be intrinsically rather than extrinsically motivated (prompted by our own sense of meaning and enjoyment as opposed to that of our parents or our culture); they must be harmonious (rather than conflicting with one another); they must satisfy innate human needs (such as the need to be an expert at something, to connect with others, and to contribute to our communities, rather than simply desiring to be rich, powerful, beautiful, or famous); they must be aligned with our own authentic values; they must be reachable and

flexible; and, ideally, they should focus on attaining something rather than evading or running away from something. (Lyubomirsky, 2013, p. 241)

The pursuit of worthwhile goals is a practice that increases our sense of meaning and provides a deeper source of happiness. It is a source of meaning that is available to all of us and when we have selected a worthwhile goal, we can begin by breaking it down into daily or weekly aims.

Teaching offers us many possibilities for pursuing meaningful goals and for experiencing that satisfaction and ease we feel when we help our students and colleagues. This help may be in the form of empathy, acts of kindness, thoughtful listening, sharing ideas, or creating metaphors that spark new insights and support learning. When it comes to enjoying greater happiness, it helps to know that we do not have to make a choice between helping others and helping ourselves. In fact, research has shown that altruistic people are happier. They take pleasure in witnessing the happiness of others and in this way become happier themselves.

In synthesizing the research on happiness, Ben-Shahar (2007) says, we "enhance our happiness to the greatest extent when we pursue activities that provide us with meaning and pleasure *and* that help others [original emphasis]" (p. 127). In these ways, we are creating happiness in our life and in our teaching that is sturdier, more consistent, and longer lasting.

Some Questions to Ask Are:

- How aware am I of the small pleasures, activities, places, and people that make me happy?
- Are my mind and heart telling me that I should be doing something differently, spending my time in better ways? Is my heart telling me I must change an important part of my life?
- What are my passions? What are my strengths? How am I incorporating my passions and using my strengths in my teaching life?
- What contributes to happiness in our school – both ours and our students? Is it possible to expand beliefs about what makes us happy and become more aware of what contributes to the happiness of our students?

Some Practices to Consider Are:

- Visualize your future happiness and successes in detail. Visualization activates the same parts of your brain as actually carrying out the activities, which is why this has become a powerful tool for winning athletes, high-performance musicians and dancers, and others. Research demonstrates that it can be both a positive and an energizing practice.[4]

- Cultivate a loving concern for others and notice your acts of kindness. Take a moment at the end of your day to revisit the ways you were considerate of the feelings of your students and colleagues. Great happiness comes from the quality of your relationships with others.[5]
- Dialogue groups: Reflect together on all those things that are sources of happiness in daily life. Decide individually on one, small thing you could do in the day that would contribute to your happiness. Share your choice with others, commit to incorporating it, and at a later date, share what you experienced as a result of incorporating it into your day.

Thoughts to Remember

Everyone can have a happier life despite their circumstances because in some ways happiness can be "learned" and many studies have confirmed this and described practices that can be adopted for creating a happier, more meaningful life. You can be that happy person whose pleasure in life is contagious – spreading the happiness bug to your students and others in your life.

An important foundation for a happy life is believing that we are worthy of happiness and becoming more aware of what makes us happy. We need to have a broad concept of happiness that includes a range of positive emotions and many sources of meaning. Our happiness can shift over the long term when we believe in our emotional sturdiness and recognize that we have good coping skills. Happy people notice and are grateful for small pleasures, take pleasure in helping others, and pursue worthwhile goals – enjoying the process more than the achievement.

NOTES

1. The concept of happiness as being a synthesis of pleasurable experiences and an overall sense of meaning and direction is found both in the fields of psychology and philosophy. This chapter is grounded in sources that synthesized the contemporary research and centuries of thought related to happiness. For example, works used from the field of positive psychology which offer good summaries of the research related to happiness include Ben-Shahar (2007), Fredrickson (2009), and Lyubomirsky (2008, 2013). Lenoir's (2015) *Happiness: A Philosopher's Guide* provides an accessible synthesis of philosophic thoughts related to happiness over the ages and from many countries.

2. This right to happiness is explained well in Ben-Shahar (2007), pp. 144–45.

3. See for example, the work of Seligman, Steen, Park and Peterson (2005) and Seligman (2011).

4. Cooperrider (1990) demonstrated the effectiveness of positive visualizations in his research with managers in organizations, and Fredrickson (2009) confirmed and described its broader application.

5. The work of Dutton (2003) also confirms this finding from positive psychology and suggests other practices which contribute to a happier workplace. See her book *Energize your Workplace: How to Create and Sustain High-quality Connections at Work*.

Chapter 24

Experiencing Joy

> He who binds to himself a joy
> Does the winged life destroy;
> But he who kisses the joy as it flies
> Lives in eternity's sun rise.
>
> —William Blake

The eighteenth-century poet William Blake is considered by many to have been a visionary, seeing and writing about the life of the spirit in a broader and deeper way than most of us understand our life to be. Where we may see limits, he saw possibilities, angels in the trees, and heaven in a wild flower. His insight here is a central one in terms of how we live joyous moments. We try to be fully present to them and then we let them go, knowing that joy cannot be willed nor captured. When you experience joy in your teaching, it can permeate the classroom atmosphere and offer students a feeling of freshness in the very air they breathe. Hearts are lightened, however momentarily.

Odier (2014) describes the path to joy as a part of the life search for meaning and the extent to which it involves wholeheartedness and creativity.

> Joy does not tolerate half measures. One cannot be partially joyous. . . . Joy implies creativity and the courage of freeing oneself from many of our own concepts and conditionings. One can only access it through steadfast fearlessness. (p. 3)

We create the conditions to experience joy when we let go of all pretensions and presumptions in order to be vitally present. We attend to the moment with the mind of a beginner seeing and hearing the world for the first time. This seems a tall order in the classroom. We approach the possibilities for joy in the learning environment when we are comfortable with students as they are and support their self-expression. When we want our classroom to come alive with enthusiasm for the ideas and processes we explore, it is important to diminish the effects of judgments and comparisons.

This happens when we are focused on students and their engagement in learning rather than external standards and testing unrelated to classroom learning; and when we create a community of learners rather than a competitive atmosphere. Alfie Kohn has been visiting classrooms across the United States for decades looking for those conditions that create vibrant learning environments and asks us to remember the happiness that is lost through grading, ranking, and narrow forms of testing. He uses the language of joy when he says,

> Anyone who has spent time in classrooms that vibrate with enthusiasm needs to keep such memories alive in all their specificity to serve as so many yardsticks against which to measure what we've lost: six-year-olds listening to a story, rapt and breathless; teenagers so immersed in an activity that they forget to worry about appearing cool; these little explosions of delight attendant on figuring something out. (2011, p. 150)

The freshness of joy as Kohn describes it is in students being fully present. We can experience this ability to be fully alive and enchanted with life as teachers and as humans. Can we imagine and enjoy feeling, hearing, and seeing each moment as part of the process of the unfolding universe – knowing we are part of this unfolding? In Odier's view, joy stems directly from our presence in the world and involves our ability to embrace the broadest area of reality at our disposal. In good times and bad times, we remember and allow ourselves to be influenced by what is often called "the big picture."

Richo (2005) calls this an unconditional acceptance of the givens of life including that everything changes and ends. He says that saying "yes" to all that life offers up to us is a way to a spiritual and sane life. We are acknowledging that whatever happens to us is useful on our path. In Richo's words, "When things change and end, we become trusting of the cycles of life as steps to evolutionary growth. When things do not go according to our plans, we stretch our potential for trusting a power beyond our ego" (p. 101).

He continues his description of the unconditional "yes" to life as a path to happiness by suggesting that when things are not fair, we can renew our vow to act fairly and when people are not always loyal and loving to us, we can renew our commitment to acting with compassion. Richo feels that following this way of being leads from happiness to joy.

> There is a vitality in us, a sparkle – a bonfire, actually – that cannot be extinguished by any tragedy. Something in us, an urge towards wholeness, a passion for evolving, makes us go on, start over, not give up, not give in. To accept the

things we cannot change does not mean that we roll over but that we roll on. Openness and creative resourcefulness happen synchronously each time we are confronted with one of the givens. Some people write their best poems when they suffer. (pp. 102–3)

Spretnak (1991) offers another perspective on joy as the grace that comes from our sense of connection and feeling of unity with all of life, an experience of being embedded in "the sacred whole that is in us and around us." She says, "At such moments, our consciousness perceives not only our individual self, but also our larger self, the self of the cosmos. The gestalt of unitive existence becomes palpable" (p. 24).

> *I remember the joyous feeling I had when I was walking along the lakeshore early one morning. A group of little shore birds were hurrying along ahead of me on their long spindly legs. I ran. They ran faster. I laughed. The freshness of the morning and this simple experience of closeness to the birds was a gift of my presence. In Thoreau's words, I was "awake."*

Rachel Remen is a doctor who has learned a lot about fulfillment in life from her work with patients who have cancer. She describes her concept of joy in relation to these experiences.

> I had thought joy to be rather synonymous with happiness, but it seems now to be far less vulnerable than happiness. Joy seems to be a part of an unconditional wish to live, not holding back because life may not meet our preferences and expectations. Joy seems to be a function of the willingness to accept the whole, and to show up to meet with whatever is there. . . . It is the lover drunk with the opportunity to love despite the possibility of loss, the player for whom playing has become more important than winning or losing. . . . Joy seems more closely related to aliveness than to happiness. (1996, pp. 171–72)

People experience joy when possibilities expand. A moment such as when Barack Obama won the presidency brought joy to many black Americans who saw their own histories validated and their futures enlarged. Another situation where joy may be felt is when the world itself expands. Powerful images from the Hubble website show us the universe in its enormity and fierce beauty in a way that captures the spirits and imaginations of many humans – joy is felt in being part of the mysteries of the cosmos.

One way to bring together the ideas expressed here in relation to finding joy in life is to look at this path as one of giving up on the idea of being in control. We accept that because everything is connected to everything else, much of life is unpredictable and unknowable. We act with creativity and love. We find peace in knowing that we are striving to become fully human and present to our daily life and whatever it offers. In this way, we see and feel more deeply and our spirit is enriched. This allows us to teach from a joyful place.

Some Questions to Ask Are:

- In what ways do my experiences of joy depend on the strength of my presence in the world? Do my feelings of joy increase in moments when I am fully present, and do they decrease when I am distracted? How does this affect my teaching?
- To what extent do I feel myself to be whole hearted and non-judgmental? Do I understand how these qualities might contribute to experiencing joy?
- Do my joyous moments seem dependent on certain objects or people or do they stem from a deeper, innate source?
- Do we see a connection between joy and courage, and between the absence of joy and the need to control everything that happens in our classrooms?

Some Practices to Consider Are:

- When experiencing joy, consider the source and how it can be used to enrich your personal and teaching life.
- When dealing with stressful or sorrowful events, notice where the joyful part of your self is residing. See if you can touch base with this "alive" part of your self – that part that feels connected to the universe.
- Dialogue groups: Make it a group focus for a week to notice joyful moments that occur in your teaching day. Think about and discuss how these moments affect your teaching and the learning of your students.

Thoughts to Remember

Joy is different than and less vulnerable to the ups and downs of life than happiness. Joy is an orientation to life where you feel connected to everything in the universe with your whole body, mind, and spirit. You are not separate, you are part of the glorious whole from the amoeba to the swirling galaxies, and experiencing this is a way to be fully present and awake.

One way to bring together the ideas in relation to finding joy in life is to look at this path as one of giving up on the idea of being completely in control. It is a path of accepting what we cannot change and acting with creativity and love to change what we can. It can take courage to remain fully present to all that life brings us, but it is in that complete engagement that moments of joy happen. When we experience joy in our teaching, it can permeate the classroom atmosphere and offer our students a feeling of freshness in the very air they breathe.

Part IV

TO STRENGTHEN OUR BONDS WITH OTHERS, AND THE NATURAL WORLD

Good teachers possess a capacity for connectedness. They are able to weave a complex web of connections that join self, subjects, and students in the fabric of life. The connections these teachers make are held not in their methods but in their hearts.[1]

NOTE

1. A paraphrase of Parker Palmer's thoughts about the ways good teaching comes from the teacher's ability to develop strong bonds with students, colleagues, and the world around them and use their understanding of interconnectedness to create curriculum and an environment that supports learning (1998, p. 11).

Chapter 25

Teaching with Kindness

> Accepting students for who they are – as opposed to for what they do – is integrally related to the idea of teaching the whole child. That connection is worth highlighting because the phrase "whole child" is sometimes interpreted to mean "more than academics" which suggests a fragmented education. The point isn't just to meet a student's emotional needs with this activity, her physical needs with that activity, her social needs with something else, and so on. Rather, it is an integrated self to whom we respond. It is a whole person whom we value. And to do so in any way that matters is to accept children unconditionally, even (perhaps especially) when they screw up or fall short. (Kohn, 2011, p. 120)

Following Kohn's reasoning, genuine acts of kindness would come from a teacher who is a whole, integrated person bringing all aspects of her/his being into classroom relationships. Our kindness is strengthened and grows out of our ability to also see those we teach as whole persons and not simply as students.

Kindness comes in many forms and incorporates other virtues including fairness, forgiveness, and generosity of spirit. The generous spirit of teachers is exemplified in our willingness to give recognition when it is due, to show appreciation, and recognize the accomplishments of others. With this generosity we give our time, energy, and understanding; and use our creativity to foster the independence of students and others in our daily circle of life.

When students feel safe in our classroom and in our care, they are freer to focus on their learning and their learning improves. Research that supports this crucial relationship between students' emotional safety and their learning comes from many fields including De Steno's (2014) important synthesis of studies, confirming that a learner must trust their teacher to learn from them (pp. 76–77).

A foundation of trustworthy and caring relationships begins with knowing our students and supporting them to grow and change. Seeing our students with open minds and hearts also means we are sensitive to changes in their demeanor which might tell us they are struggling with something difficult or hurtful. With this attentiveness, we may more readily know when someone needs help and be more aware that it is not necessarily someone from the group of students who are struggling academically. Kindness requires responses that are sensitive to students' need for support and for privacy. We can show appreciation to our class as a whole and recognize individuals in quiet, one-on-one ways.

We can be more attentive to students' individual needs by not having too many preconceived notions about them or limits on ways that they can be themselves and participate. An important way to show our interest and enjoyment of our students is to encourage their questions and remarks – being more open to the surprising, intriguing, or profound and insightful things our students say. Exploring students' ideas and questions together can deepen the learning of everyone, and appreciating their unique viewpoints and humor relaxes students and motivates them to participate more fully and genuinely. Students feel they are valued when we support them to pursue their interests and take ownership of their learning.

One of the greatest acts of kindness we can offer to our students is to demonstrate our belief in their intelligence and inner goodness.

> *It is a real tragedy when young people feel they are failures. Often this starts when they believe in labels such as "bad," "stupid," "ugly," "slow," or "poor." Whether or not these are spoken aloud, classrooms are often places where students intuit which students such labels fit. Marking practices and grouping practices reveal classroom rankings for better and most often, for worse.*
>
> *For this reason, I start my year with each new class by talking honestly with them about damaging labels and the harm they do, and especially that they are never true. I tell them, "You are all good persons, whether or not you have ever acted in unkind, selfish, or thoughtless ways, you still have goodness in you. You have a good heart that no one can ever take away. The goodness inside you is permanent and you can always use it to become an even better person."*
>
> *The other message I made sure all students receive is, "All of you are smart. Even when you have trouble learning something, it doesn't mean that you are what some people call dumb. Dumb is a very ugly word and it is never true. Everyone is intelligent and has gifts. Not everyone is smart in the same way. There are many ways to be smart." Then I teach them multiple intelligences theory, and in several cases, I witnessed this having a profound effect on a student's morale and subsequent learning.*

> *I like to start and end the day with some variations on these messages or with questions that demonstrate how much I value their input. I use questions like, "What is one thing you want help with today and where might this help come from?" and statements such as "I enjoyed being with you today and appreciated all your creativity and good humour."*

However, showing consistent kindness toward all students is not easy. Actions in the classroom that we later regret often happen in the heat of the moment. For this reason, teachers need a simple touchstone, one that can be easily remembered and quickly drawn upon in the moments we have to decide how to react. What we need to do in these moments is have a way to evaluate potential responses. Some good ones to use are: Would it be kind? Would it be helpful? Would it lead to greater student independence? Is the way I respond a behavior I would like students to learn?

The essence of kindness is acting in ways that contribute to long-term benefit to students – that is, supports them in taking more responsibility for their future, and models a way to respond to others that is kind and helpful. Kindness refers to fair, empathetic, and compassionate behaviors. Helpfulness refers to teaching a valuable life skill, supporting greater independence, and respecting students' abilities to learn, change, and grow. An example of a life skill would be starting a response to a disruptive behavior by first telling the student/s that you know they are good persons. Confirm that you care about them, then ask for the behavior you would like to see. Kindness can be as simple as showing an interest in our students' interests and life beyond the classroom.

A deeper aspect of kindness, one that does not necessarily take the form of words, is the feeling we have sometimes of empathy or compassion for a student who is struggling with some kind of challenge. If we see our students through the eyes of the heart and believe they are all sacred beings with a role to play on earth, we deepen our care and empathy for them and they will feel our support even without our saying it out loud. Glazer's (1999) understanding of the roots of compassion and kind actions is helpful to think about here. He says,

> Compassion emerges from a sense of belonging: the experience that all suffering is like our suffering and all joy is like our joy. When we know ourselves to be connected to all others, acting compassionately is simply the natural thing to do. (p. 34)

Everything we can do to help each student feel they belong and are valued is the way we *live* our kindness and this genuine caring for their welfare and well-being helps our students to treat each other kindly as well.

Some Questions to Ask Are:

- What is my motivation for extending my regard for students beyond academic success to supporting their overall well-being?
- How do I show my interest in students' ideas, encourage their input, and support their independence?
- How do I establish good connections with students' parents or caregivers, and find thoughtful ways to learn from them about their children's interests, needs, and struggles?
- How do I model respectful and caring behaviors? Do I model important life skills as a way to support students in developing them?
- Do we show our students that we care about them as persons as well as care about their learning? How can our actions and other responses address their social, emotional, and spiritual needs as well as intellectual ones? What can we do to help all students feel valued?

Some Practices to Consider Are:

- Make a point to engage in daily acts of kindness in your interactions with students – making sure they are genuine and go beyond praise. We want students to feel we care about them for *who* they are, not simply for what they achieve.
- Develop some short practices that give students opportunities to write or talk about their interests, gifts, out-of-school activities, questions, and their worries and challenges. Make sure that all students know they don't have to reveal anything they don't feel comfortable revealing. An example would be having students write one sentence about themselves once a week, asking them to tell something different each time.
- Dialogue groups: Focus a discussion on ways to show greater kindness toward your students and activities that help them to be kinder to each other. Talk about how you can limit practices that place students in any kind of hierarchy or invite comparisons of better or worse, or weaker or stronger students. You might extend this to a discussion of all the ways you can support student engagement.

Thoughts to Remember

Treating students kindly and fairly makes it easier for them to learn. You can make your classroom emotionally safe for your students by responding in ways we would like our students to respond to others. Kindness to students also means that our responses help them to become increasingly independent – demonstrating life skills they can use now and in their future life.

Everything that we do to support students to feel ownership for their learning and help them to expand and pursue their interests is a form of lasting kindness. Practices that help us know them as persons and value them for who they are on the inside helps them to value themselves. The more care you demonstrate for their well-being, the freer they are to learn and grow and the more likely it is that they will pass the kindness along.

Chapter 26

Keeping a Sense of Humor

> I can tell *moshom* (Cree for grandfather) is pleased
> with the questions I'm asking.
> *it's time to come home!*
> *it will be a great summer*
> *after a stay at St. Paul's.*
> *nitanis,* (Cree for my daughter) he says
> *wipe those tears from your eyes.*
> *a chat with St. Peter has assured me*
> *a place for you*
> *beside me,* he jokes. I laugh,
> death is natural.
>
> (Excerpt from Rita Bouvier's "Music in My Mother's Movement" [revised 2015], *Blueberry Clouds,* 1999, Saskatoon, SK: Thistledown Press, p. 22. Reprinted with permission.)

Our busy lives as teachers often prevent us from taking the time to appreciate the humor present in our everyday lives. These humorous moments can range from a student's "ah ha" related to a learning discovery to a teacher's personal reflection related to a classroom observation. It is ironic that such daily experiences, which are often funnier and less insulting than traditional joke telling, are rarely shared as stories to bring joy and discovery to ourselves and others. It is useful to think about how our schools may or may not support the use of positive humor. Do we see individuals engaged in playful discussion or are the hallways silent tombs of long faces?

Humor helps us learn to laugh at ourselves and to laugh together. It supports us in having fun and has a way of creating bonds among people. It is healthy, it feels good, and everyone can speak this language. We are drawn to laughter and it has been medically proven to be good for our health and well-being.

From the mild to the outrageous or slapstick, humor allows us to enjoy an experience together. It can increase our trust to describe a blooper we made, or by letting people know what makes us laugh and what we find to be funny. In addition, it allows us to explore an experience more deeply or, perhaps, differently. Sharing positive, humorous experiences can also increase our confidence to use humor to mitigate difficult situations. In all situations, using humor in positive ways requires a degree of higher order thinking.

Humor has two meanings. It can be thought of as the mood of being in good humor and a positive frame of mind, or the ability to see the funny side of life and share it with others. It has been described as an ease of manner, openness, and friendliness. Other qualities that support humor are the ability to see the humorous side of life and remain cheerful including collegiality, sociability, fairness, and being relaxed and comfortable with who we are. With a nature tuned to humor, we feel appreciation for the accomplishments of others rather than competitiveness.

Many of us have experienced tense or stressful situations, where our sense of humor is noticeably absent. Taking a moment to be present with the situation and to remind ourselves that we are whole, complete human beings (which includes having a sense of humor) is critical to being able to engage the skill of using humor in appropriate ways to defuse a tense situation. Well-placed and timely humor can dissolve frustration or anger and allow individuals to continue to participate in tense or difficult situations in order to solve problems or to hold critical conversations. Having a moment of comic relief allows us to lighten up and not take ourselves so seriously in the midst of a difficult situation. Humour, if used skilfully, can support involvement and solution finding in tense situations as well as help build community in a group.

There are a few times when humor is not an appropriate response. An example is when we let our humor drift into sarcasm as a way to appear clever or to belittle someone. We can use our self-awareness to ensure that a humorous remark is not unkind or insensitive to human diversity. We can also check in with our bodies and hearts to make sure we are not hiding behind our humor when what is really needed by another is to respond thoughtfully to their expressed need.

Humor can be used to debrief the stresses of the day with someone who cares about us. However, we want to guard ourselves in these situations from using humor to feed our cynicism in relation to such things as the unfairness of an administrative directive. With awareness of these cautions, we are freer to give our humorous observations to others and receive theirs in return.

Enjoying spontaneous humor with our family, students, and colleagues helps build community moment by moment. Each shared funny experience builds trust and strengthens the bonds of community. These experiences do not need to be planned. Some of the best times are those where we take advantage of the topic of a lesson or conversation to recall a funny incident that is related to it.

This might be from our knowledge of history or literature, other times it might be from our own life, or from a cache of appropriate jokes that we have collected over the years. Students love to enjoy a laugh in the middle of a lesson that is challenging. Research confirms that sharing a story or joke that is relevant to the content of a lesson can increase the likelihood of the topic being understood and remembered (Lundberg & Miller Thurston, 2002; Jonas, 2009).

Humor can increase our well-being by decreasing our tendency to feel anxiety or tension when a practical task isn't going well. Can we laugh at ourselves at times where we might otherwise be frustrated? One example is where we catch ourselves in the middle of a ridiculous experience that becomes too funny for words or a task that we have complicated beyond measure until we discover the shortcut. How many of us have changed a printer cartridge for the first time and ended up sweating and covered with ink until, at the end of the 20-minute process, we discover that a simple push and pull would have removed the spent cartridge in less than five seconds!

It is wonderful when we can let go of the frustration and allow the spontaneous experience of humor to pervade the moment. One way to let go is to stop and take time to appreciate the humor in the situation and to recall it after the fact in order to regale our students, colleagues, family, and friends. Another way is to take a picture, jot down a note, or talk to other people who are present to mark the occasion and plant it more fully in your short-term memory.

Sharing our humor in kind and thoughtful ways with our students helps them to see us as individuals who have the same types of experiences as they and the people in their families do. It can help them see how humor can be used to recover from a hurt or to look at life in a different, more enlivening way. It somehow helps to make us more human in students' eyes when they see that we have the ability to appreciate the small surprises and pleasures of everyday life. It also allows them to realize that we are more than our work life, more than a teacher. We are a person with ideas, feelings, and a sense of humor that can be used to enrich their experiences. This is a realization that students don't always reach.

One way to ensure the recall of funny events in relation to our teaching life is to write a short description at the end of the day of the event that occurred in the classroom. This ensures we have a memory bank of humorous moments to enjoy again and to share with others. We can also use them to create community in the classroom by asking our students to relive a funny event, *"Remember when Jimmy brought his rubber boots to school that a skunk had sprayed and he told the story of how their dog had caught the skunk and flung it at him? Jimmy had us rolling in the aisles because his story was so funny."*

Focusing on the humor in everyday life, and engaging others in this focus, is a balanced and healthy way to develop feelings of happiness and strengthen connections with others. This source of happiness and strength is freely available and can feed our spirit so that we continue to enjoy our rewarding and challenging lives as teachers. When we begin to look for the humor in daily life, it is surprising what we notice.

> *Every winter, our village ploughs the snow from the street in front of the post office and forms a pile at the corner of the driveway into the local hotel. As I was walking to get my mail one sunny winter afternoon, I saw a golden retriever dog madly digging in this pile of snow. As he sent the snow flying, he was creating rainbows in all directions. When I facetiously asked the owner if her dog was looking for a bone in the snow pile, she laughed and said, "I don't know what it is about this pile of snow! He does this every time we walk by it!" I still smile when I think of this dog wildly digging in this pile of snow just for the joy of it!*

One might argue that nothing is funnier than everyday events. These include the questions and observations of young children which, while often being insightful, can be incredibly funny! Similarly, an earnest conversation with a colleague can end in exaggeration or turning things upside down, leading to deep and uncontrollable laughter and joyful tears! If we are open to seeing and sharing the humor in everyday life, we will deepen our experience of what it means to be human while enriching our enjoyment of teaching.

Some Questions to Ask Are:

- Is it possible to see more humor in everyday life? How can I do this?
- What have I recently experienced in my daily life that I have shared (or could share) as a humorous, joyful incident?
- In what ways have I used humor to build community?
- When have I used humor to defuse a situation?
- Is positive humor a common occurrence at our school? Do we want it to be a common occurrence at our school?

Some Practices to Consider Are:

- Take a moment to appreciate the humor inherent in a situation and let your inner appreciation develop into an external smile.
- When a humorous incident crosses your path, take the time to appreciate the moment and recall it later to your family, friends, or students.
- Dialogue groups: With your colleagues, discuss all the ways that humor helps us get through a difficult time, enjoy life, create a memorable classroom moment, or when you have been able to point out the humor in a situation as a way to build community or to release tension. See if any of your colleagues' strategies might work for you as well.

Thoughts to Remember

Everyone is capable of being funny, making others laugh, and seeing the humor in everyday occurrences. Focusing on seeing the comic side of human life helps us to be more alert and awake, playful and accepting of what can't be changed – turning it around for our amusement and to entertain others.

Humor that is not unkind or cynical creates strong bonds with those we care about including our students. Using our humor in the classroom can help students see us as whole human beings and model alternate ways to respond to frustrations or setbacks. It can be used to defuse stressful situations and debrief stressful events by exaggerating them out of your tense body and into shared laughter. Invite your students to use their humor and help them to see what joking is appropriate and what is not. In this way, you are encouraging them to relax, be themselves, and use their creativity. What a good way to warm the classroom atmosphere and support learning!

Chapter 27

Cultivating a Classroom Community

> Some jobs are too big to handle alone, or simply more fun when done with friends. Either case leads us into the fruitful and challenging field of collaboration. Artists working together play out yet another aspect of the power of limits. There is another personality and style to pull with and push against. Each collaborator brings to the work a different set of strengths and resistances. We provide both irritation and inspiration for each other – the grist for each other's pearl making. (Nachmanovitch, 1990, p. 95)

Although Nachmanovitch is referring to artists in the quote above, his ideas apply equally to our classrooms. We are building communities of collaborators which bring both joy and challenge. An important benefit in providing students with the security to expand their horizons and explore the plentiful nooks and crannies of our world is knowing that they are not alone and can count on their fellow explorers to support them. These explorations are strengthened through conversations, games, and other activities that our students do together. At their best, classroom communities offer the security for members to explore their respective worlds while developing deep and supportive relationships.

A community, in its strongest sense, is more than a collection of individuals. It is a living whole, an interconnected group of persons who share a common goal, work together to achieve it, and understand that this takes kindness and mutual support. Creating a caring learning community in the classroom is, perhaps, the most important and valuable work a teacher does. It supports all students to learn more and become stronger and kinder than would be possible in a competitive, hierarchical environment.

Personal qualities that help teachers develop a sense of community in their classrooms and schools include kindness, sensitivity to the feelings of others, imagination in relation to picturing and understanding the realities of others, and commitment to provide a holistic education – one that supports the body, mind, and spirit. Our fairness in caring equally about all our students and our trustworthiness in being reliable and consistent in what we say and do give students a sense of security and help them to relax.

Without a sense of security in classroom life, students find it difficult, if not impossible, to learn. Teachers cultivate a classroom community by providing a safe environment in which to learn, by showing an interest in students' lives and in students as persons, by helping students to understand the importance of supporting each other's learning, and by increasing their sense of belonging. See Appendix C for a sample plan to nurture students' feelings of belonging.

A natural action that stems from the appreciation of our students is to acknowledge the ways we enjoy teaching them and appreciate their efforts. This can be done in class time and with the class as a whole. In addition, being on the lookout for positive things to acknowledge about individual students and, if appropriate, to the student's parents/caregivers, can be done privately so as to diminish any type of competitiveness between students. When the recognition and appreciation of all students' unique qualities is our orientation toward teaching, over the year or semester, it is possible to discover many things to affirm and enjoy. There is a lovely sense of satisfaction that comes from increasing the happiness of our students – one of the most basic rewards of the teaching life.

Another way to increase our students' sense of belonging is to learn about their interests and express a corresponding interest in what they know or do. This may encourage students to open up and share their knowledge, not only with us but also with other students. By expressing some interest, we can show the other students that their classmate is worth spending time with and listening to. Cultivating a classroom community requires that we build relationships not only with our students but also among our students.

Taking time to explore with our students what it means to be a community is a rewarding exercise that can help to strengthen students' sense of valuing and caring for the learning of their classmates. Poet Stanley Kunitz in Burstein (2011) describes the fundamental insight we and our students need about the way everything is connected to everything else.

> One of my deepest concepts is that the web of creation is a continuous tissue whose invisible filaments envelop every living organism. All of us are connected, are related. If you touch the web at any point, if you disturb it, the whole web trembles. (p. 63)

By emphasizing that the behavior of one class member (including the teacher) affects all of the class members, we are teaching a valuable life lesson. This is also an important understanding for creating a community within the staff of a school.

Classrooms have an atmosphere which can be sensed as relatively full of tension or feelings of ease. To create an environment in which students feel safe to be themselves and open to learning we need to take their social, emotional, and spiritual needs into account. A sense of community is developed and strengthened when class members see each other as having the same human emotional, social, and spiritual needs and know each other as individuals of worth. (See Appendix D for ways to develop understanding of emotional and spiritual needs.)

In addition, positive shared experiences build a memory bank of the class as a community that enjoys being together. Collecting these experiences entails supporting students to interact in kind and productive ways. This can be achieved through prior preparatory experiences, explicit teacher modeling and guidance, and other strategies. Sometimes it is helpful to have students plan for upcoming experiences through imagining the needs and feelings of everyone involved.

Last year, we had a new student join our group midway through the semester. The week before the new student was to arrive, I asked the students to write a letter to the new student (in their journals) that would describe a fear that a new student might have along with a reassurance that the fear was unfounded and why. On the day following the journal writing, I had the students (in small groups) make a list of the fears that had been described in their letters and discuss why such fears would not be realized.

In discussing the small group lists as a class, we discovered many similarities across the lists and were gratified to know that all fears could be mitigated by the way our classroom chose to help the new student feel welcome. We ended the discussion by having individuals volunteer to "buddy" with the new student on each day of the school week for the next few weeks.

These types of preparatory activities help students to draw on their own experiences in empathizing with the position of another. They also prepare students to act in more thoughtful and caring ways. Over time and with guided experiences, students tend to become more skilled at noticing and supporting positive aspects of others, and more patient at dealing with trying aspects.

Helping students to see a range of ways of being or preferences supports them in understanding why others may behave differently. Often the diversity that is the hardest for students are those related to gender, sexual identity, race, culture, and language. These take sensitive and, sometimes, explicit teaching using story and film. An important aspect of this caring for all students and helping them to broaden their acceptance of others is to teach students to look beneath the differences and see the ways in which others are just like them in wanting recognition, support, and friendships. By showing and modeling kind and respectful behavior, and being specific about what it looks like, we can help students learn to act from the heart with skill and grace. In a sense, everything becomes a teaching moment and every member reaps the rewards of building a classroom community.

To achieve the ethos of a safe and caring environment, the energy in the classroom needs to be positive and to flow freely. In classrooms where this occurs, there is a synergy that is created among the students, the teacher, and the subject matter under study. This synergy holds a learning space where teachers and students breathe life into the classroom and the topic under study.

Within this sacred space, the teacher and students can explore and enjoy making sense of the world through disciplinary and interdisciplinary lenses. In a synergistic learning space, we can better support individual learning needs and interests. As a teacher, your heart will be full every day when you focus on cultivating a classroom community where individuals feel safe, supported, trusted, and valued.

Some Questions to Ask Are:

- What personal qualities do I have and which ones could I strengthen in order to build relationships with students and cultivate a community of learners?
- How do I ensure that the classroom is a safe and comfortable place for me and the students to take risks and to learn?
- How do I support students to get to know and enjoy their classmates, to respect their feelings, and to understand that they all have the same needs for safety and recognition?
- To what extent do I feel connected to my students, the classroom or classrooms in which I teach, the objects in my teaching context, or the resources I used and the lessons I plan? In what ways might the strength of connection to my class and their learning support students' sense of belonging and community?
- How can we focus on enhancing those teacher qualities that will support us in developing communities of learners in our school? How can we build the interpersonal skills of our students to interact positively and productively with others?

Some Practices to Consider Are:

- Change membership of working pairs and small groups regularly so students have an opportunity to work with all members of the class, over a semester or school year. It is when students spend time with each other, through supportive and productive processes, that they have the opportunity to discover each others' finer qualities.
- Celebrate successes, even small ones, as a large group. Support students in acknowledging each others' progress and, in particular, the progress of the entire class in relation to learning and to community building.
- Dialogue groups: Use the chart in Appendix D with your school staff, teacher reading group, or a few colleagues to reflect together on the ways everyone's emotional and spiritual needs are met by their teaching life. You might also use it to discuss this same focus in relation to the student body.

Thoughts to Remember

A classroom community values the diversity of its members, seeks unity in its overall goals, and acts from the understanding that the behavior of one can affect the feelings and behavior of all. The metaphor of a web is a strong image for understanding both the strength of the connections and the fragility of humans' feelings in relation to being accepted and valued.

We can foster a sense of belonging to a learning community by being interested in our students and helping them get to know each other's interests and strengths – a knowledge that is supported by your own kindness, fairness, and expectations that students also embody these virtues. Empathy, patience, and a light touch, when dealing with the personal domain, are community practices to model and support. The benefits of having a caring, compassionate, and nonthreatening classroom atmosphere include greater academic learning and personal growth for our students and increased pleasure and professional satisfaction for us.

Chapter 28

Supporting Teacher Voice

> Concerned about our own need to belong and to feel worthy – concerned to create a better world from the sometimes chaotic materials of everyday life – we now have to work harder than ever to make our voices heard, to make our desires real, to bend events to our ends.
> (Kingwell, 2000, p. viii)

For Kingwell, to shape the world we want, we need to be able to speak up as global citizens. This allows others to know what we think and perhaps provide another viewpoint as we contribute to the dialogue underway. Finding our voice can be challenging but *is* worthwhile, not only for ourselves, but for others and for the world. Democracies and communities become stronger when all voices are heard.

Sometimes, it is the support and encouragement of others that allows us to find our voice and contribute to the communal conversation. When we are able to tap into our center and speak our truth, words don't fail us. We are knowledgeable about what we think and what we care about. Bringing our voice forward allows us to contribute to the broader discussion. If we believe our contribution will strengthen the learning of our students or support a fellow colleague, this can give us the courage to speak up.

Schools offer many challenges when it comes to contributing to group processes or decisions. It can take a courageous and concerted effort to do this, particularly if we have been ignored in the past or if our ideas have been rejected out of hand. There might be times in meetings or personal conversations where tough decisions need to be made, and surly or upset individuals make it difficult for us to find our voice. Knowing we have the support of a colleague certainly helps. This can increase our confidence to insert ourselves into the conversation and face the risk of being visible.

Often it is the school ethos that makes the difference in teacher participation. It can be instructive to notice how teachers *use* their voice. A teacher can be a strong community-builder just by the ways she or he is a genuinely warm and positive human being.

> *I worked in the same school for several years with someone I felt was a master teacher. If Jean told us a funny story about one of her students, she always left you with the impression that the student was bright and capable and never a problem. When Jean went to a conference, even when her participation was required rather than voluntary, she would come back with new ideas and appreciative comments about some of the speakers.*
>
> *Jean was usually quiet in meetings – waiting until everyone had had a say before sharing a thought or two. Two things made her contributions especially valuable. She only spoke when she had something constructive to offer and her thoughts seemed to always uplift rather than dispirit others. I experienced myself changing the ways I participated as a result and noticed the overall atmosphere at coffee breaks or meetings was more congenial when Jean was present.*

Not all schools have teachers like Jean, but all of us can learn behaviors that bring people together and support fuller participation. One place to start would be to improve the ratio of our appreciative or humorous comments over critical or defensive ones. Expressions of gratitude almost guarantee that the speaker is heard.

When we find our voice and are willing to take the risk of speaking our mind, it can be valuable to draw on strategies that allow our voice to be heard and our ideas to be considered. Rosenberg (2003) promotes compassionate or nonviolent communication as a technique to transform conflict into mutually satisfying outcomes. He suggests a four-step process where we:

1. observe what we see or hear,
2. notice how we and the speaker feel,
3. sense the need that is causing these feelings, and
4. articulate a clear request in relation to the need.

Noticing how we or the speaker feel requires empathy – the ability to listen "with our whole being" (p. 91). When we believe we are truly being heard and our feelings are being acknowledged, it is easier to discover the common ground from which solutions can be found.

Finding common ground or committing to a common vision that transcends ourselves encourages the human spirit to come forth. An example follows.

A teacher was able to inspire other staff members to contribute to efforts to improve the playground through demonstrating the benefits to students' health and well-being that would accrue. By using Rosenberg's technique of compassionate communication, he was able to garner support. It was the physical needs of the students and their future joy on the playground that motivated this teacher to voice his ideas and inspire his colleagues.

As a classroom teacher, it is easy to feel overwhelmed and undervalued when arbitrary decisions are made at the school, district, or regional level. These decisions usually have an impact on school ethos, classroom workload, and student learning. Haberman (2004) and others note the negative stressful effects related to lack of teacher participation in decision-making at the school level. While many administrators include their staff in problem solving and solution finding, it is helpful if we, as teachers, also develop strategies together to support the inclusion of our voice in school decisions.

> *When the school district decided to bring in a single reading programme that all students from Kindergarten to Grade 3 had to participate in, the teachers at my school were very concerned. We had a wide range of student needs at our school and we were adopting and adapting practices from several reading programmes depending upon the needs of our particular students.*
>
> *Three of us got together after the initial announcement and prepared a strategy for the upcoming staff meeting where we supported each other in raising specific student examples of where the new reading programme would not be as effective as the current, individualized approach. The other teachers supported us and the principal agreed to talk to the district office regarding flexibility in accommodating and adapting the new reading programme so that students' needs would guide how best to integrate the programme.*

Although administrators are usually tasked with introducing new policy or directives, it is often more constructive when teachers participate in figuring out how best to apply these directives at the school level. In the teacher story above, it was the strategic planning prior to the meeting that opened the door to thinking about other ways to accommodate the school district directive. As teachers have the intimate daily contact with students and close relationships with their respective family communities, it follows that teachers possess the relevant and practical knowledge and experiences to offer in strengthening or changing school processes, and developing workable solutions to school issues.

In any discussion or problem-solving process, it is equally instructive to consider whose voice is not being heard. Everyone benefits when all voices are heard, any personal concerns listened to, and a diversity of viewpoints raised for consideration. Sometimes listening to colleagues and helping them to find a way to clearly voice a concern at a meeting or express empathy in a personal situation is what is needed. Taking time to help individuals find their own voice strengthens not only the life of the school but their personal lives as well. See Appendix C for a sample plan and follow-up related to supporting teacher voice.

The range of teacher backgrounds, interests, and strengths available in a school has the potential to provide a strong base for developing communal solutions to troubling school problems or for creating new programs or events. Working together to include the voices of all can ensure stronger ideas and strengthen collegial relationships.

Some Questions to Ask Are:

- Am I aware of the predominant forms my communication with colleagues takes?
- How can I focus on connecting through empathic listening even under trying conditions?
- Can I find more ways to make my contributions appreciative, funny, supportive or encouraging of others?
- How can I raise concerns in ways that better ensure that others will listen at the school, community, and school district level?
- How can we strengthen teacher voice in making decisions at the school and school district level?

Some Practices to Consider Are:

- Use your understanding of the ways that all humans need recognition to show genuine appreciation of your colleagues for work well done or suggestions they make in meetings. Teachers are more likely to voice their opinions and ideas when strengthened by the encouragement or advocacy of their peers.
- When school community or staff meetings become heated due to differing viewpoints, it is helpful to step in and ask "what can we agree on?" In this way, the group's attention focuses on common ground which changes the energy of the discussion and, hopefully, opens the door to discovering mutually agreeable solutions.
- Dialogue groups: With your networking group, brainstorm various strategies for raising concerns during staff meetings and parent teacher association meetings in respectful and constructive ways. Discuss sensitive ways to offer to be part of solution-finding processes, and to encourage peers to do the same.

Thoughts to Remember

Everyone wants to be seen, heard, and respected just as no one wants to be disregarded when it comes to decisions that affect them. We need to be involved in problem solving and idea generating particularly because we work on the front line of education and know more about the needs of our students, ourselves, and our colleagues than those more remote from daily classroom life. Sometimes, we need support to find our voice and bring it forward.

There are many ways to support greater teacher voice in decision-making and the creating of better schools, and all ways depend on respectful relationships and empathetic listening. Important touchstones for use in resolving conflicts that arise are those of remembering that the school is a community where the actions of one affect the feelings of all and where individuals embrace the practice of seeking common ground.

Chapter 29

Sharing and Learning with Others

> One of the most underused resources available to educators is the community of colleagues with whom they work. Such communities are invaluable when they work well because a great way to learn and develop as a professional is to do so in partnership with others who are doing the same thing. (Caine & Caine, 2010, p. 1)

Teachers benefit from the opportunity to learn from and be supported by their peers. A large body of research exists that demonstrates the importance of trust, enjoyment, and social support from colleagues and coworkers. Some of this research[1] indicates that empathetic and constructive support from teachers' peers is the most important preventative factor in teacher burnout.

Such support can be informal or formal in nature. It can be given in intimate one-on-one conversations or in structured small group discussions. These groups can be comprised of individuals who teach the same subject(s) or the same grade(s) or a more diverse group interested in learning and growing, both personally and professionally. There are many possibilities for group sharing and learning.

For example, does the group want to discuss issues arising from their teaching, brainstorm responses to school district requests, compile a central pool of resources, engage in inquiry learning, or focus on other areas of common interest?

While my teaching degree is in secondary education, an opportunity arose in my second year of teaching to teach in my home community. This meant that I would no longer need to commute on icy, winter roads to the neighbouring city

> school. I jumped at the chance to teach at the school in the community where I lived even though it meant I would be teaching in a multigrade classroom. I was grateful to the director of education who introduced me to the other teachers in our school division who taught in the same multigrade situation as me.
>
> Early in the school year, we formed a networking group where we shared teaching strategies for multigrades, engaged in "make and take" activities, discussed our challenges and successes in multigrade situations, celebrated our personal and professional accomplishments, and became close friends. In this way, I became part of a supportive professional learning community while expanding my repertoire related to teaching and student learning and exploration.

Before forming a group, it is helpful to think through the expectations for sharing, learning, and building trust. To support any sharing and discussion, it is important that the group decide on the purpose for networking and adopt norms for generating agenda items, supporting the participation of all group members, ensuring the respectful treatment of individuals and ideas, and other aspects that contribute to effective and productive groups.[2]

It is important that each member of the group has an opportunity to contribute to the discussion and decisions, and to benefit from the sharing and learning processes. The informal sharing in staff rooms and hallways also benefits from these norms. Even a short exchange between two colleagues can be an opportunity for mutual support and professional learning.

> In my first year of teaching, I was lucky to be placed across the hall from a seasoned teacher. We both taught grade 8 students and used the same reading programme. He would often stop and stand in my classroom door at the end of the school day and share something he was planning to do with an upcoming story in his drama period. I tended to try out his ideas in my classroom and they were always successful in that they broadened my repertoire of how I interacted with my students and the types of activities that I was willing to try in my lessons.
>
> As all of my teaching background had been dedicated to teaching a second language at the high school level, I was very grateful to this teacher for his generous spirit and we became lifelong friends. Because of this experience, I always made an effort to share my teaching ideas and materials with other educators. One of my fond memories of teaching is the close collegial friendships that I made in the various schools where I taught.

The most important personal guideline for teacher support groups might be that members offer each other mutual reassurance and nurturing of the spirit. One example of this nurturing is the way the group responds to stressful events. It would mean that the group is clear that while debriefing stressful events and sharing worries, fears, and anger at injustices in their school system could play a role in group meetings, it must not be the main focus of sharing. Sharing stresses is beneficial only when it is met with empathy and leads to mutual solution finding.

Collegial groups can spiral downwards as well as lift teachers' spirits. Negative emotions are more easily transferred than positive emotions and negative events and feelings tend to be stronger, last longer, and are remembered longer than positive ones. As well, negativity narrows our vision and limits our thinking while positive thoughts and emotions have the opposite effect.[3]

Guidelines for networking sessions can be developed to maintain a warm and positive atmosphere – one that empowers its members to feel they can overcome challenges and continue to grow as teachers and as persons. In these sessions, we experience an increase in energy as we draw on the empathy and expertise of others in our professional learning community. The research of Caine and Caine (2010) shows that a healthy learning community reduces teacher stress.

In some cases, the school ethos may not be conducive to sharing and learning with others or perhaps the district does not coordinate teacher networking sessions. School cultures differ. Where some schools might have a focus on professional learning, other schools may not offer these types of opportunities. In these situations, it is important to support your peers and also look to your peers in finding opportunities to network.

When we face challenges together and openly welcome differing perspectives, we come closer to exploring the heart of the topic and to discovering what we really think. Sometimes we discover a novel idea together. Networking sessions can turn into learning communities that focus on issues of personal interest and provide opportunities to reflect and to ask questions. When networking, we notice the emphasis on listening, dialogue, and taking action. These opportunities allow us to personalize ideas while enjoying time spent with each other.

Personal qualities that support sharing and learning together include trust, empathy, respect, open-mindedness, and a positive focus. When we believe in and respect the principle that all teachers have knowledge and gifts to offer, sharing becomes a way of life. While teacher networking and dialogue groups can fulfill our yearning for deep connection, they also provide a space for building theory from practice which, in turn, leads to strengthened teaching and improved student learning.

It is important to create discussion spaces that are open and trustworthy – such spaces allow for deeper dialogue about what it means to be a teacher. According to Parker Palmer and colleagues (2001),[4] these spaces must be simultaneously hospitable and intellectually challenging. When networking sessions are conducted in respectful ways, teachers are more comfortable challenging themselves and others with heartfelt and thought-provoking questions.

Some Questions to Ask Are:

- Am I aware that teachers, like all humans, are sensitive to social comparisons and work to ensure that my comments support and value differences?
- How can we help beginning teachers feel comfortable asking for help and advice?
- How can we share ideas and lessons, contribute to school assemblies, and create hallway displays without increasing a sense of competition among staff members or of inadequacy in an individual teacher?
- In what ways do we support silent reflection in our professional learning community so that group members can enjoy an opportunity to think, to calm themselves, or to experience group solidarity?
- Are there other ways in which we can build trust, support each other, and enjoy our teaching life to the fullest? What can we do if our school culture makes this difficult?

Some Practices to Consider Are:

- Find ways to strengthen bonds with your colleagues. For example, you could go out once a month for lunch as a small group or with the entire staff. These occasions offer opportunities for sharing stories about personal lives and getting to know each other in a different way.
- With your colleagues, work to diminish comparisons and any sense of competitiveness.
- Dialogue groups: Devote one or two of your sharing time sessions to the question of how the group can develop practices that turn a staff into a collaborative team who share resources, ideas, and mutual support.

Thoughts to Remember

Teachers need social networks with other teachers in order to learn more about effective teaching practices and receive more personal and professional support. This form of support, when entered into with caring and respect for each other, is a potent stress reducer and confidence booster.

Important guidelines for teacher sharing, whether one-on-one or in groups, are to encourage every voice, to remain open to all topics that individuals want help with, to empathize with the feelings expressed, and to adopt a problem-solving stance in relation to negative events that have been experienced. The bonds between colleagues that are formed in this way make the school environment a warmer, happier place for everyone.

NOTES

1. Larrivee (2012) summarizes the results of a large number of studies that support this conclusion.

2. For ideas regarding dialogue, sharing, and problem solving in teacher groups, refer to *Classroom Curriculum Connections: A Teacher's Handbook for Personal-Professional Growth* (Saskatchewan Education, 2001).

3. Westman (2001) and Fredrickson (2009) confirm these effects of negativity.

4. Caine and Caine (2010) confirm this and argue that the overall atmosphere needs to be one of relaxed alertness combined with high intrinsic challenge.

Chapter 30

Seeking Nature, Outside and Indoors

> It is not so much for its beauty that the forest makes a claim upon [hu]mans' hearts, as for that subtle something, the quality of air that emanates from old trees, that so wonderfully changes and renews a weary spirit.

The poet Robert Louis Stevenson wrote these words over a century ago and his insights were based on his own experience. Scientists today confirm these benefits not only to the human spirit but also to the mind and body.

Research from many countries and for over 100 years has consistently demonstrated that contact with the natural world can help to improve mental functioning, elevate mood, relieve stress, calm the mind, and help to alleviate insomnia. Spending time in natural settings also has been demonstrated to lower the levels of the stress hormone cortisol, and reduce psychological stress, depression, and hostility.[1] Even viewing nature scenes on television or a computer or through a window can lower blood pressure and heart rate. Research has shown that nature therapy strengthens the immune system and speeds recovery from illness or surgery.

Nature therapy also has mental, emotional, and social benefits. Taking breaks outdoors during staff meetings can often result in meaningful conversations or "aha" moments. Children and teenagers' concentration improves after a short walk outdoors. Similarly, taking students outside will allow them to engage in meaningful experiences and to use their senses differently. It is interesting how time spent outdoors interacting in some way with the plants, animals, wind, water, sand, or earth can strengthen our relationship to the people with whom we share these interactions. We create shared bonds and shared memories.

Nature is also a wonderful source of the beauty that our heart craves. While trees and plants may beautify our surroundings and calm our mind, they also reduce pollutants in the air, indoors and out. The negative ions that are found in abundance in forests and near bodies of moving water have been shown to increase our antioxidant defense system. Studies of the ways in which urban parks with a variety of trees and shrubs contribute to the well-being of people who regularly spend time in them are well documented in Selhub and Logan's (2012) extensive review of the research.

> In a study published in 2009 in the Journal of Health Psychology, among almost 550 urban men and women, higher scores on the connectivity to nature scale were associated with greater overall psychological well-being, vitality and – very importantly – meaningfulness. (p. 227)

When walking in public parks or gardens, it is important to open your heart. Large gardens and parks rarely show you everything at once. Gardeners like to surprise you with different views. When you round a corner in a garden, you may be surprised by something. In this way, gardeners mimic nature.

> *I often review students' journals over the weekend. I like to take a break after an hour or two and walk along the creek in our village. My regular walks along the creek path offer me a surprise each week. I find sunlight is always good for my soul and I enjoy the changing ways it illuminates the landscapes I walk through or the distant views I see.*
>
> *In the spring, I smell and see a new flower blooming and other flowers fading each week. There is a symmetry and synthesis of new growth coming from old, decaying growth. I notice that nature has a way of surprising me around every turn in the path, no matter the season. I also enjoy how being out in nature calms and refreshes my mind so that I can go back to my work with renewed clarity and energy on my return.*

Time spent in nature can create deeper bonds with the other than human world, bring feelings of peace, and elevate the spirit.

Fortunately, there are many ways to experience the benefits of nature including:

- Walking in forests
- Spending time by, on, or in naturally-occurring bodies of water (lakes, rivers, oceans, waterfalls, bogs, ponds, streams)
- Sitting or walking in a park, with a variety of trees and other plants, which is home to many birds, insects, and small animals

- Watching birds, butterflies, and dragonflies in a variety of green spaces, including your own yard
- Gardening outdoors or incorporating plants into your indoor environments
- Viewing the sky, trees, and other natural phenomena through a window or skylight
- Watching animals in their natural habitats, from squirrels and rabbits to bighorn sheep
- Being outdoors on a sunny day, sitting by a sunlit window, or using a blue light box in winter or on gray days
- Listening to tapes/CDs of bird songs and other sounds from nature
- Viewing nature scenes on a computer or television
- Aromatherapy using natural ingredients such as extracts of lavender, rosemary, or jasmine.

The general rule, developed from synthesis of research focused on the various forms of nature therapy, is that the most benefits accrue from actually being outside in green spaces that contain a high degree of biodiversity including coniferous trees. As Selhub and Logan (2012) remind us:

> It is not possible to cultivate true concern and empathy for nature while being completely detached from it. True connectivity in any relationship, be it interpersonal or with elements of nature, serves to strengthen empathy and concern. (p. 55)

Perhaps the greatest gift that comes from time spent outdoors is your feeling of being at home. This feeling creates a bond with the natural world which we can draw upon throughout our life. Spirits can be strengthened and joy in life increased by a wealth of experiences in and with the natural world.

Some Questions to Ask Are:

- Where are the natural settings close to my home and my school? Are there nature preserves within easy driving distance in my area where I can spend a day on weekends and holidays?
- What lessons could I plan to ensure that I and my students reap the many benefits of nature therapy?
- What psychological or practical concerns might be limiting me from spending more time outdoors? Are there small steps I can take to transform or remove some of these concerns?
- In what ways do I notice the natural rhythms of nature reflected in my personal life and my teaching life?

- How can we show that we value nature in our school, our schoolyard, and the surrounding community?

Some Practices to Consider Are:

- Assess the strength of your bonds with the natural world by taking the quiz, "How connected to nature are you?" (See Appendix E.) Use this knowledge as a base for strengthening your sense of connection.
- Enliven your senses and experience awe by viewing storms – appreciating all their power and drama.
- Dialogue groups: With your colleagues, brainstorm how your networking group might become an advocate for the planting of trees and gardens in school yards and urban neighborhoods.

Thoughts to Remember

Extensive research has confirmed and described ways in which spending time in natural settings benefits the body, mind, and spirit. The strongest benefits from nature therapy come from spending time outdoors in natural settings with a degree of biodiversity.

Treat yourself and your students often to the calming powers of natural settings, the gifts of nature's beauty, the stimulation of all the senses, and the opportunities for awe and wonder. In this way, we are strengthening our and their comfort level and bonds with the natural world and all the life it contains. In a sense, we are reminding ourselves and teaching our students that in nature we can experience solitude without feeling alone, and feelings of solace and peace as well as stimulation and pleasure.

NOTE

1. Books such as those of Selhub and Logan (2012), Louv (2005), Beresford-Kroeger (2010), and Robbins (2012) document and describe this extensive body of research related to the benefits to humans of time spent outdoors and in natural settings.

Chapter 31

Knowing the Earth Knows Us

> Some ancient native traditions believe that the world feels our seeing and sees us right back, even the trees and the bushes, even the rocks. And certainly, if you have ever spent a night alone in the rainforest or the woods, you will know the quality of your seeing and of your being is felt and known by more than the human world. (Kabat-Zinn 2005, p. 200)

We are all a part of the natural world. We come from the same building blocks as other life forms on earth and in the expanding cosmos. We may set ourselves apart from the natural world; but we are not apart, and when we do not remember this, we are diminished, the planet is harmed, and we are closed off from rich sources of learning, growth, and enjoyment.

As teachers we have the potential not only to enrich our own lives by a deeper understanding of the aliveness of the natural world and the ways it communicates with us but also to share some of this potential for enrichment of daily life with our students. Like all humans, we and many of our students feel sad and alone at times. To develop the ability to feel known and be part of the trees, plants, animals, and stars would give us and our students a sense of belonging that once felt cannot be taken away.

Coleman (2006) describes the rewards of opening our hearts to other living things as another way to be in love.

> When we attune to nature with sensitivity, we can see just how connected we are. Falling in love with a meadow, a limpid stream, a young fawn, or a grove of oak trees does not happen without those things "reaching out" and touching us in some way. We are always in relationship; we just rarely notice it. From this perspective, everything on this earth, from the spring rains that provide fresh

drinking water to the warmth of the sun, is an open-hearted, generous offering. To wake up to this idea is to realize how abundant our lives truly are, how we receive gifts of love from nature all the time. (pp. 9–10)

To be genuine in offering more of nature's gifts to ourselves and our students, we need to be outdoors more often and strengthen our presence and our ability to feel the presence of the other forms of life around us. This practice of listening and sensing more deeply can become a source of pleasure, a solace when we need it, and assurance that we are not alone.

When my life partner died, I was bereft and spent many hours weeping. The one place where I felt safe to fully express my grief was during my morning runs. As snowflakes would fall on my tear-stained face, I knew in the deepest part of myself that mother earth was large enough to hold my sorrow and would, at the same time, keep me whole – holding together the thousand pieces of myself that threatened to fly out of me as I wept uncontrollably. This daily "communion" with the earth on a visceral level allowed me to survive the initial months of being alone.

Indigenous cultures are aware that nature is aware. They say, "The earth knows us." When they have lived in the same habitat over centuries, they say, "Here nature knows us." This is a lovely idea for reflection – to understand beyond an intellectual level that the earth is alive and communicates with us, and accepts us, perhaps even remembers us. This requires a different kind of knowing and the understanding that there are different forms of consciousness – both within us and within other forms of life. Sometimes our language restricts our ability to know aliveness beyond the human world. Sometimes it is our lack of experiences in natural or wilderness settings, or that our imaginations are constrained by our fears or habits.

The more deeply we know the natural world around us, the more likely we are to see the ways non-human living beings respond to our presence and speak to us. We may see the idea of the earth speaking as metaphor or we could understand that there are many ways to communicate. When humans walk the same route for many years, the plants respond by drawing back and our route becomes a path. The earth knows our footsteps.

This path is an example of our profound interconnection with all other life forms on earth – the air, the water, the plants and animals, the mountains and minerals. The trees around us evolved from the earth and we evolved from the earth and we are together in this evolving. We might try to know this in a way that the tree knows it. To enrich our lives in this way requires developing a consciousness beyond that which gets us to work every day to a larger and deeper consciousness that participates in the universe as a knowing, sensing part.

Two aspects of deepening our consciousness of the aliveness of the earth are to develop all our senses to a greater acuity, and to use the power of our imagination to recognize that there are many ways that living things can communicate with us. They may speak in song, like numerous birds, in rustling like the leaves, or in rhythm like the ocean waves. But, as Abram (2011) reminds us, the primary purpose of any language is to draw us into relationship – into the "vital presence of the world."

> The power of language remains, first and foremost, a way of singing oneself into contact with others and the cosmos, a way of bridging the silence between oneself and another person, or a startled black bear, or the crescent moon soaring like a billowed sail above the roof. (p. 57)

Among the shamanic traditions of American Indians and Eastern Europeans, "power" animals are seen as a gift from the Creator. They are considered to be spiritual guides that speak to us through visions, dreams, and wild animals that we meet in nature. In their physical form, wild animals remind us of our connection to all of creation and, if we let them, can help us to understand our direction in life. With an awareness of this ancient teaching, and if we remain open to the messages of animals in nature, we may learn things of significance to our life. Trees and other plants also spoke to men and women all over the world – revealing to them the medicine they held (Beresford-Kroeger, 2010).

Kathleen Winter (2014) describes how profound the communication between the earth, sky, plants, and animals can be when we are prepared to dwell in and on the earth in a deeper way and for longer periods of time. Her perceptions of this communication came when she was in the Arctic on land and on a ship moving through what Europeans called "The Northwest Passage."

> I knew I'd come deep into a presence of an Arctic majesty that possessed no trappings, no charts, no commandments on stone. It spoke no audible word, yet I heard its message and felt a current. A communication from the earth had begun to infiltrate me in a way that was different from how I normally intercepted things. Here, in the waters under my rocking bed and in the land around us, hummed communication – a message in the combined body that broke my solitude and connected me with the North's living energy. (p.161)

If we take the time to be open, the landscape, plants, and animals that we meet in nature have a message for us. The challenge is to pay attention. Simply to bring our attention to the air as it moves in and out of our nostrils and to know that we share that air with the tree as it breathes and the frog as it croaks are ways to understand that we share the earth and are enriched by this knowing.

Some Questions to Ask Are:

- In what ways am I connected to the non-human world we call nature? Do I find natural phenomena as sources of meaning, beauty, comfort, solace, inspiration, anxiety, or annoyance? For example, is the sky a weather forecaster, a work of art, a book that I read every day?
- Are natural phenomena only the background to my human life? Can I see them as participating in my life, as relationships and interactions affected by my presence and behaviors, as I am affected by theirs?
- Does developing greater understanding of the ways the earth knows us also increase my appreciation of the wisdom and consciousness of traditional indigenous cultures?
- In what ways might I support my students to become more aware and appreciative of the natural world and notice how it might be communicating with us?
- Are there places we find to have a sacred quality offering us peace and restoration? In what ways do we experience them as speaking to our soul?

Some Practices to Consider Are:

- Think of all natural phenomena as having ways to communicate with you in their own form of language. What are their messages to you?
- Spend time walking outside every day – the slower pace fosters your own sense of connection to the life around you.
- Dialogue groups: Focus one of your times together on the benefits we receive from feeling connected to and known by other living things. Share stories of times when nature was a solace, an inspiration, a teacher, or when it spoke to your heart and mind in some way that was healing.

Thoughts to Remember

The earth is alive and full of life forms that came from the same source as you did and are communicating with you. You can learn how to listen, see, and feel their messages and be enriched. The wonders of the universe of which you are part can cause you to feel humble and awed – two emotions that heal and sustain us and lead us to protect rather than destroy other life forms.

We can help students experience the power of belonging to all of life and being in communion with other living things through teaching them to go out in the world with their senses alert, their imagination active, and their hearts open. When we use this same practice, it enlarges our sense of self and confirms that we belong here, and are never alone; we are a part of a great and wondrous whole.

Chapter 32

Extending Kindness and Compassion to All Beings

> If the boundaries of the self are defined by what we feel, then those who cannot feel even for themselves shrink within their own boundaries, while those who feel for others are enlarged, and those who feel compassion for all beings must be boundless. (Solnit, 2013, p. 107)

We have come full circle. Our explorations of ways to strengthen our spirits and nourish our overall well-being create new possibilities for us to be open to the earth and all its creatures and cultures. The sense of belonging and connection this creates enlarges us as humans as we develop an openness of heart and empathy for the suffering of others, including the plants and animals in the oceans and on the earth. We also experience the joy of other humans as our joy and the well-being of plants and animals as our well-being.

It is a wonderful and enriching place to attain – the viewpoint that celebrates the human and biological diversity of our world and understands that we are a part of it with a role to play. When we are present to it, we can be an appreciator, a participant, a nurturer, an actor in creating a better world. Compassion is a gift that motivates us to contribute to the greater good and rewards us with the feelings of mutuality and sharing in the sorrows and joys of our life with others.

With this attainment, we are never alone. All the pleasures and struggles of human life are not foreign to us. We see into the hearts of those who are struggling, angry, even destructive, and we can wish for them a better life. We watch the sunrise, the birds in flight, the weeds in our lawn, the mosquito that landed on our arm, and even when we don't always appreciate their role in our life, we can accept that all these forms of creation are needed in some way as part of the balance that makes life on earth possible.

The Dalai Lama expressed this best when he said in response to being told that many people in the west feel unworthy and are very self-critical, "But that's a mistake. All beings are precious!"[1] We might use this statement of the preciousness of all living beings as a central meditation, reflecting on all the ways that this is so. Knowing that we have a role to play in maintaining the health of the earth, and creating the common good, is a reason to love ourselves.

Robbins (2014) describes the link between appreciation of ourselves and appreciating other people in a meaningful way.

> When we authentically appreciate ourselves, we give ourselves permission, perspective, and awareness to look for, find, and see the inherent beauty and value in other people. Once we see this, we can express it. When we have the courage to express our appreciation in a generous and genuine way, it can literally transform our lives. . . . When we expand our capacity for appreciation of others and of life, what we're really doing is expanding our capacity to appreciate ourselves and, in so doing, we become more available for the love, connection, and fulfillment that we desire. (pp. 95–96)

There are many ways to extend this love and compassion to other people – those we meet, those we read about, those we watch on television.

A wonderful practice created by Chade-Meng (2012) is called "Just Like Me"[2] which consists of the reminders that every person has a body, mind, feelings, and emotions just as we do. Everyone has at some point been sad, hurt, disappointed, angry, or confused just like us. Everyone has suffered physical and emotional pain just as we have. And everyone wants to be healthy, happy, and loved as much as we do. With this understanding, it is easier to wish individual persons well – to wish that they have the inner strength and emotional and social support to survive and do well despite the difficulties of life.

As so much of our daily life is influenced by the way we think, another way of extending compassion is to make kindness a mental habit – your default mode. This is a form of neurosculpting that can (when enacted genuinely and repeated often) become an instinct for kindness. You can use this on your daily walk, bike, or drive by wishing every living thing you pass, a person, a dog, a blade of grass, "I wish you to be healthy" or "I wish you to be happy." The Buddha taught that what one thinks about frequently becomes an inclination of their mind. In regularly thinking and wishing kindness for others, we become a more loving and compassionate person.

> *It has taken me a long time to face the suffering in the world and the human causes of much of it. It is often hard not to despair in the face of destruction of the environment and human destructiveness and cruelty. I think feelings of*

> *helplessness have a lot to do with my wish to avoid knowing these aspects of human reality. I find that if I make a commitment to know about the situations that are causing suffering – either of humans or other life – by watching the television programmes that document their stories, I find faces full of dignity, sensitivity, and human goodness and acts of generosity and courage.*
>
> *Even when I can't help directly, I can feel great compassion for the suffering of others and this compassion transforms how I respond to the people I meet in daily life. The other practice I have is to know what my role is in creating a better world and often find the answer in my teaching. I am committed to teaching about the suffering and the goodness of humans and the importance of compassion and kindness. One of my messages is, "Kindness starts here in this classroom."*

Purpel (2004) places our ability to contribute to the common good through our teaching and in the face of many challenges as coming from spiritual strength and says,

> Let us as educators, citizens, and human beings have faith in our ultimate commitment to the creation of a just and loving community. Easy to say, hard to do. Unless we take into account our amazing human capacities and that mysterious spirit that is the source of that faith that energizes and inspires them. (p. 280)

There is much suffering, unfairness, even cruelty in the human world. There is also much kindness, generosity, courage, and altruistic behaviors. It is helpful to understand these compassionate actions as natural behavior of human beings and not as unusual or remarkable. Mordecai Paldiel,[3] who is involved in humanitarian work in Israel, says we have a tendency to distance ourselves from the good acts we witness while at the same lauding the altruistic behavior of others. Paldiel asks, "Would it not be better to rediscover the altruistic potential within ourselves?"

When we believe in our potential for compassion and kindness to all beings and act on it in simple ways every day, our world and our classroom become a better place. Through participating in our commitment to alleviate suffering and act with compassion and kindness for those in need, our students learn perhaps the most important ability of all – to think and act with their hearts, and gain the essential understanding that they are needed and have goodness at their center.

Some Questions to Ask Are:

- Do I know the limits of my ability to feel compassion and care for others including other forms of life?
- Does my kindness and understanding of the needs of others come from a deep source that ensures the actions that follow are genuine?

- Have I used the understanding that comes through honoring my pain and grief as a motivation to reach out to others, to become a fairer and kinder person, or to work for greater social justice?
- Can I face and empathize with the suffering of others in the world (e.g., when witnessing the large scale suffering caused by famine and war)?
- Do we help our students develop the understanding that kindness begets kindness and that compassion is contagious?

Some Practices to Consider Are:

- Start each day with the reminder that all beings are precious.
- Use the idea that others have suffered and want to be happy just like you to expand your understanding of others and your capacity to wish even those whose behavior upsets you happiness and greater well-being.
- Dialogue groups: Explore ways in which you can work together to grow genuinely kind habits of behavior in your classroom, staffroom and school community. Discuss ways to ensure that kind acts come from compassionate hearts and not as the result of coercion, praise, or rewards.

Thoughts to Remember

Teaching is a profession that has great potential to contribute to the common good. Extending compassion and kindness to others feels good and these acts spread out like ripples in a pond, encompassing wider circles and more living things. Your capacity to face the suffering of others, wish others well, and help when help is needed is always there, and each small action strengthens your altruistic potential and encourages you to greater kindness.

Appreciating ourselves, our basic humanness, and the ways we rise to daily challenges, enlarges our ability to appreciate others. The understanding that all living things are interconnected and that the behavior of one can affect the behavior of all is a foundation for thoughtful actions and a motivation to develop greater feelings of compassion and care for other people and all sentient beings.

NOTES

1. Described in Kornfield (2008), p. 27.
2. For a full description of his "Just Like Me and Mindfulness Meditation," see Chade-Meng (2012), pp. 168–69.
3. As quoted in Ricard (2015), p. 119.

Parting Thoughts

There are only two ways to live your life.
One is as though nothing is a miracle.
The other is as though everything is a miracle.

—Albert Einstein

Whether you have taught for one year or thirty years, you will have discovered that teaching is not for the faint of heart. Every day, we witness miracles with our students – the first time they kick a soccer ball, experiment with their voice in song, or tackle a difficult physics challenge. This is the way to live our teaching life – on full alert experiencing the joy, pain, success, and frustration that learning brings. Teaching is a profession that promotes authenticity, courage, and spiritual aliveness. It is a serious vocation where we affect the lives of others – our students, their families, and our colleagues. To bring our soul energy forward in this rewarding endeavor, a valuable question to regularly ask ourselves is, "What would I do in this situation if I truly loved myself?"

For all of our children, we want their teachers to be comfortable with themselves in the universe; to know that their students bring different gifts to the classroom that are yet to be discovered; to find joy in quiet, contemplative moments and in noisy, messy experiments; and to make decisions for the good of all. This way of being brings together knowledge of the head, heart, and gut to access deeper knowing. When we connect at the level of integrating our head with our heart and gut instincts, we find a type of balance where we can bring greater insight to our teaching life. From this integrated position, it is easy to see the holistic nature of our students and the pivotal role we play in ensuring that their spirits are not damaged as they learn about the world around them.

It is rewarding to guide our teaching journey with a sense for the highest good we wish to achieve through our teaching and to continue to explore and remind ourselves what we want the meaning and purpose of our teaching to be. The central message of this book is that the more we invest time, energy, and thought into personal growth, the more rewards we will reap in our life as a teacher. To be fulfilled as a teacher, it is vital to strengthen our relationships with ourselves, our students, our colleagues, and the natural world. Dedicating ourselves to improving the quality of these relationships is really a way to bring more love and strength to the way we view and experience our world.

The harmony we achieve between our teaching responsibilities and self-care will be the measure of the long-term satisfaction we receive from our teaching. Opening our mind and heart to learning along with our students, becoming more curious about other life phenomena, and keeping our sense of wonder alive will support our spirit and will inspire our students to greater learning.

Finding individuals, groups, or experiences that support you in thinking deeply about teaching and learning will remind you of the soulful work that you have chosen as a teacher – work that is meaningful and aligned with your heart.

Appendix A

Mindfulness

A Short Primer

> The overall tenor of mindfulness practice is gentle, appreciative, and nurturing. Another way to think of it is "heartfulness." (Kabat-Zinn, 1994, pp. 6–7)

This short overview of mindfulness is based in the works of many long-time teachers and scholars in the field who adopt approaches that are helpful to everyone. Sources used remain within a secular approach to mindfulness and mindfulness meditation including Chade-Meng (2012), Germer (2009), and Kabat-Zinn (1990, 1994, 2005). As well, a book that is particularly useful to teachers is Schoeberlein's (2009) *Mindful Teaching and Teaching Mindfulness*.

The approach to mindfulness described in this appendix was developed originally at Harvard Medical School by doctors and other therapists for use in their Stress Reduction Clinic. While Kabat-Zinn and his colleagues developed mindfulness meditation drawing on ancient traditions of self-inquiry and healing, their focus was on its uses in holistic medicine rather than as a spiritual or religious tradition.

They wanted to support participants in the Stress Reduction program to develop a loving wholeness – a shift in the ways they thought of themselves and in the ways they responded to pain and stress. From the beginning, research was part of the context at the clinic and findings showed its benefits so clearly that it became a part of some programs in other fields including psychotherapy and education.

MINDFULNESS IN DAILY LIFE

Mindfulness is the act of paying attention, on purpose, in the present moment and nonjudgmentally. It is a practice of enacting kindness to the self, moment by moment. This attitude of kindness is a foundation of the ability to be awake and aware. Mindfulness is not about getting somewhere else in your thoughts, feelings, or body, but being fully where you already are. It is a way of knowing what you are experiencing while you are experiencing it or of keeping your consciousness alive to the present reality. It can also be understood as a way of looking deeply into oneself with openness, in the spirit of self-inquiry. With mindfulness, the mind observes itself. Thus, it is a form of meta-attention or attention to our attention.

In this sense, it can be an informal and momentary experience of being aware and knowing what is happening. This attentiveness can be achieved when washing the dishes, eating lunch, reading to your child, or other daily routines. Perhaps you have experienced moments of mindful attention in your classroom. Through paying attention more closely, we may become more aware of our thinking as it accompanies our actions.

We might then discover the tendency of our thoughts to be more often in the past or the future than in the present, and that our thoughts often distract us from noticing much of what is happening around us and inside us. We learn that we miss many moments of our life by so often being somewhere else in our thoughts. When we can focus on what is happening inside us and around us with clarity and a lack of judgment, the present moment liberates us from our preoccupations and can be very entertaining and informative.

Even the shortest moment of mindful attention can be helpful. There are no limits to the ways we can incorporate mindfulness practices into our life including forms of mindfulness meditation. In all situations, the important feature is the degree of self-compassion and commitment you bring to it.

WHAT WE LEARN FROM MINDFULNESS PRACTICES

With attention to our thoughts and feelings, we discover that we most often judge everything in relation to its value to us. We categorize some people and things and events as "good" and others as "bad" and ones that have little importance to us are considered to be neutral and hardly noticed. We like some things and want more of them. We dislike other things and want them to go away.

This tendency to judge, based not necessarily in reality but in our personal preferences, locks us into habitual reactions that can rule our days. Our thoughts overwhelm our perception of the present moment. When judgments dominate our minds, it is difficult to have any peace. It is also the case that you often don't see the people in your life with fresh eyes, and as they really are at that moment. Rather, we only see our thoughts about the person – our version of this person formed by our previous judgments. We could say that we see much of our reality through the veil of our opinions.

WHY IS MINDFULNESS HELPFUL?

Mindfulness helps us to notice how the mind works and to develop a more harmonious relationship to our thoughts and feelings. Through commitment to being present, without expectations for what the experience should be like, and gently bringing our attention back when the mind wanders, we learn to calm down enough to become more deeply relaxed. Mindfulness nourishes our body and mind and helps us to see the ways we actually think and feel and live.

Through mindfulness, we learn our thought patterns, where we are tense and tight, what we really value, and who we are underneath the daily stresses and responsibilities of our lives. It is a simple process but it is not always pleasant and easy to accept the parts of ourselves that are revealed by paying attention. Mindfulness is not escape from emotional pain. Paradoxically, when we learn to notice and accept our pain, it calms us down. Mindfulness makes space for our pain and can bring us new insights into its roots.

With the awareness that comes from mindfulness, we more accurately identify our own feelings and those of others. This supports the development of greater emotional intelligence and the likelihood that we will reap the benefits of being more emotionally attuned.

Research has shown that a mindfulness practice strengthens the immune system. It can also reduce our tension or anxiety. Through dwelling in awareness, we can easily observe that every aspect of our experience comes and goes. Our thoughts, feelings, and the sensations in our body change from moment to moment, waxing and waning, even disappearing, including our experience of physical and emotional pain. Insight into the impermanence of experiences can be freeing.

In each moment, we practice self-acceptance and self-compassion because these moments are the only time we have to accept and calm ourselves gently, kindly. Over time, we come to know a part of our self that is trustworthy, strong, and as close as our next breath, and one that is not dependent on our particular life circumstances. This recognition and the strengthening of our awareness make our experiences more vivid and real. Germer (2009) describes this as the ordinary becoming extraordinary. For example, the drop of dew of the rose petal contains a rainbow and the taste of a raisin is unique.

When we give up our tendency to judge each of our experiences and allow ourselves to just be present to them, we begin to see the ways that we are not in charge of everything that happens. We see that there is much of life that is outside of our control. We develop greater insight into the way our perceived reality is embedded in the life around us and within a much larger reality that we may find difficult to comprehend or imagine. We experience this larger reality in quiet moments when we transcend the worries and distractions of everyday life, and connect with our higher self to discover new realizations.

In being present to our experiences without judgment, we deepen our understanding of our interconnection with all living beings and life forms. We understand that we are a small but important part of a larger cosmos that needs our care and attention. This can result in a liberating release of the energy bound up in trying to control events. We still try to act for our own well-being and that of others, but with the greater wisdom that comes from mindfulness practices, we have more calm, more insight, and greater energy to bring to those actions.

PRACTICING MINDFULNESS

The suggestions that follow offer a few simple ways to increase your awareness and overall well-being.

Open Attention

Open attention meets any object that arrives in our mind or through our senses. We sit, or lie, or walk, and we notice whatever comes in: our thoughts, emotions, feelings of ease or discomfort in the body, sounds, sights, smells. Take an attitude of openness, inviting whatever comes to be there, and at the same time being open to what comes next. Open attention helps us notice the fleetingness of thoughts, feelings, and how everything changes – nothing stays exactly the same for long.

Noticing and Labeling your Thoughts

Noticing our thoughts can be part of an informal, momentary practice of mindfulness or of a longer, more formal sitting. It is very helpful to notice how thoughts constantly change and are just thoughts, not reality. When we can simply watch our thoughts come and go like clouds drifting across the sky, or leaves floating past on a river, we realize that we are not our thoughts. A simple way to develop this insight is to simply label our thoughts as "Thinking." We can say to ourselves, "thinking, thinking, thinking" as we notice our stream of thoughts. We notice, label without judgment, and let them go.

We can also pay attention to the nature of our thoughts, and categorize them as for example, "planning, planning" or "regretting, regretting" or "revisiting, revisiting." It is helpful to remind ourselves at the beginning of a period of mindful sitting that

- thinking is just what the brain does;
- thoughts have a natural tendency to jump around;
- we are not our thoughts; and
- our thoughts are just thoughts, not reality.

Mindful Eating

When eating, take time being in stillness and silence. Listen to the subtle signals from your body. Begin by taking a few centering breaths before you take the first bite and observe the color, arrangement, and aroma of the food. As you eat, notice the texture and taste of the food. Closing your eyes may help you focus on the flavor of each mouthful. Take small bites and chew slowly and thoroughly, savoring each bite. Notice how your body feels after each swallow. Is this food life-giving or not? Take a few minutes after your meal to sit and digest, and appreciate the food you have just eaten.

Textbox A.1   Mindfulness at a Glance

Intend well. Sit, lie, stand, or move in an alert and relaxed way. Breathe. Follow each breath. Notice distraction. Acknowledge what is happening. Label it with kindness. Gently return to the breath, the body, or the activity at hand.

Appendix B

Negative Thoughts and Common Thinking Errors

Research related to helping people improve their mood, appreciate and accept themselves has discovered some common patterns of thinking that people in the Western world are particularly prone to. David Burns (1999), building on the work of Dr. Aaron Beck and other pioneers of cognitive therapy, has identified a group of negative thinking errors that affect mood, self-esteem, and lessen people's sense of empowerment.[1] Because the way we think affects the way we feel, cognitive therapists such as Beck and Burns have found ways to help people become aware of their negative and erroneous thoughts and work to transform them.

It is helpful to know that:

- We have a tendency to have automatic thoughts running under our more focused thinking, ones that we are often unaware of until we make it a practice to monitor our self-talk – those things we think but don't say out loud.
- Negative automatic thoughts are almost always exaggerated and do not accurately reflect reality. They tend to dominate our thinking because we feel they seem so believable.

Three types of thoughts that prevail when we are in a low mood are:

1. dwelling on what we perceive to be our inadequacies;
2. holding a negative view of our world in which we see all the wrong and unfair things affecting ourselves, others and the environment and feel that there is nothing we can do in the present moments to change any of it; and
3. holding a negative view of the future in which we expect difficulties, depravations, and suffering to continue.

We can lift our mood by recognizing when we are having these thoughts and challenging them – forcing ourselves to find more positive views and remembering that positive thinking is not necessarily less accurate.

COMMON THINKING ERRORS

- *All or Nothing Thinking:* The tendency to view yourself, others, and situations in black and white categories with no gray areas. For example, the idea that you are a failure when failing in one endeavor or area only.
- *Negative filtering:* The tendency to see only the negative aspects of a situation and ignoring the positive elements. One aspect of this tendency is remembering a hurt longer than a happy experience, or dwelling on one negative outcome or experience that you felt and ignoring all other positive or neutral things that happened in that same day.
- *Personalizing:* The tendency to assume that you are responsible for negative events or other people's bad behavior rather than some external circumstance of which you are not aware. This tendency is a form of mind reading and assuming things that you do not actually know. It is also a tendency to try to change the behavior of others when, in reality, we can only change our own behaviors.
- *Overgeneralizing:* The tendency to jump to conclusions – that is, to make a broad generalization from a single incident or situation.
- *Catastrophizing:* The tendency to anticipate the worst in the future without considering other possible and more positive outcomes. Instead, you might try focusing on what positive steps you could take toward ensuring a good, or at least acceptable, outcome.
- *The "Shoulds":* The tendency to hold fixed expectations for yourself and others and judge accordingly. For example, expecting people to always treat you fairly. A person could also be weighed down by constantly telling themselves all the things they *should* do without actually doing them. Notice if you have a tendency to say or think you *should* be doing something without actually doing it – almost as if saying it is a substitute for taking action.

TRANSFORMING NEGATIVE THINKING

A helpful way to become aware of negative thought patterns is to question their validity. Jacobs (2009, p. 154) provides these ten questions to support this:

1. Is this thought really true?
2. Am I overemphasizing a negative aspect of this situation?
3. What is the worst thing that can happen?
4. Is there anything positive about this situation?
5. Am I "catastrophizing," "awfulizing," jumping to conclusions, and assuming a negative outcome?
6. How do I know this situation will turn out this way?
7. Is there another way to look at this situation?
8. What difference will this make next week, month, or year?
9. If I had one month to live, how important would this be?
10. Am I using words such as *never, always, worst, terrible,* or *horrible* to describe this situation?

NOTE

1. See Dr. Burns' (1999) classic book *Feeling good: the new mood therapy*, New York: Quill.

Appendix C

Sample Personal-Professional Development Plans

SUPPORTING TEACHER VOICE IN MY SCHOOL

- *Sample Plan:* In the next week/month, I plan to support a colleague in having his/her voice heard.
- *Follow-up:* In the last week/month, I supported a colleague in raising a concern regarding teacher displays versus student displays. The subsequent discussion acknowledged the importance of profiling student work, where possible. For the next week/month, I plan to continue to find ways to support colleagues in voicing their concerns regarding our school and school district practices. In addition, I plan to bring an article for peer discussion regarding Rosenberg's compassionate communication.
- *My plan for the next week/month:* _____

- *My follow up for the next week/month:* _____

NURTURING STUDENTS' FEELINGS OF BELONGING

- *Sample Plan:* In the next week/month, I plan to nurture a sense of belonging for each student in my class.
- *Follow-up:* In the last week/month, I ensured that each student's voice was heard, and I made a point to know my students as persons. For the next week/month, I plan to promote high levels of student involvement. In addition, I plan to show an interest in students' lives by incorporating their interests into learning activities.
- *My plan for the next week/month:* _____

_____
_____
_____
_____
_____
_____
_____
_____
_____
_____

- *My follow-up for the next week/month:* _____

_____
_____
_____
_____
_____
_____
_____
_____
_____
_____

Appendix C

OBSERVING MY OWN TEACHING

- *Sample Plan:* In the next week/month, I plan to record myself for one hour daily as I work with students in the classroom.
- *Follow-up:* In the last week/month, I listened to my daily tapes and found that each day I was able to support more student-to-student interaction rather than my usual pattern of teacher–student exchanges. For the next week/month, I plan to continue to focus on promoting student–student interaction through incorporating pair and small group work. In addition, I plan to introduce a new cooperative learning strategy – jigsaw – to my students, even though I worry that this will be a difficult process for me to guide. To support myself, I will write out the process steps before the lesson and refer to them throughout the lesson.
- *My plan for the next week/month:* _____

- *My follow-up for the next week/month:* _____

TEACHER INQUIRY: RESEARCH INTO ASPECTS OF MY TEACHING

- *Sample Plan:* In the next week/month, I plan to develop an inquiry question along with a process for exploration.
- *Follow-up:* In the last week/month, I developed an inquiry plan based on the process described in *Classroom Curriculum Connections: A Teacher's Handbook for Personal-Professional Growth* (Saskatchewan Education, 2001) to examine the happy moments in my school day and explore the possibility of increasing them. For the next week/month, I plan to engage in the inquiry process that I have outlined and share my findings with interested colleagues. In addition, I plan to begin including a weekly journal writing in my lesson planning book to capture my reflections and learning from the week.
- *My plan for the next week/month:* _____

_____
_____
_____
_____
_____
_____
_____
_____
_____

- *My follow-up for the next week/month:* _____

_____
_____
_____
_____
_____
_____
_____
_____

Appendix D

Understanding Emotional and Spiritual Needs

USES FOR STUDENTS

You can use the questions and Textbox D.1 to focus discussion with your students to help them understand themselves and their peers better and to help them understand that all people have the same needs for happiness and emotional safety.[1]

Textbox D.1   What We All Need

- We need to be listened to
- We need to be understood
- We need friends and companionship
- We need to have choices
- We need to decide some things for ourselves
- We need to feel safe
- We need to feel cared for
- We need people to respect us
- We need to feel that we are good and worthy of love
- We need to believe that we can learn
- We need to like ourselves
- We need to feel connected to the natural world and other living things
- We need to care for ourselves
- We need self-compassion when we are suffering
- We need to feel compassion for others who are suffering
- We need to feel that our life is meaningful
- We need to believe that we have a role to play in the universe
- We need to feel that we are contributing to a better world
- Other needs?

USES FOR TEACHERS

The questions and Textbox D.1 can be used for individual reflection and would also provide a good focus for you and your colleagues to use in a dialogue circle in relation to how well everyone feels these needs are met through their teaching.[2] As well, discussion among teachers could focus on the challenges that students face in having these vital needs met and ways you could help.

QUESTIONS TO STIMULATE THOUGHT AND DISCUSSION

- What do you need in order to learn difficult or new things?
- What do you need when you feel lonely?
- What do you need in order to express yourself or use your creativity?
- What do you need in order to be yourself?
- What do you need in order to feel peaceful?
- How important to you is the need for privacy, quiet, or beauty?
- What do you need in order to lift your spirit?
- When you feel neglected, what do you need?
- When you feel misunderstood, what do you need?
- When you feel sad, what do you need?
- When you feel angry, what do you need?
- When you feel helpless, what do you need?
- What are all the things that humans need in order to feel safe and happy?

PROCESS FOR TEACHERS

- As individuals, you might read through the questions and look at Textbox D.1 to choose a focus for your reflection on your own emotional and spiritual needs.
- In your teacher discussion group, you might want to use Textbox D.1 to help assess the school climate and how well your teaching life meets important emotional, social, and spiritual needs.

NOTES

1. Adapted from a lesson in Finney (2013).
2. You will notice that some questions and needs relate more to students than teachers. When using them with your teacher group, pick and choose those your group wants to discuss.

Appendix E

How Connected to Nature Are You?

Rate your strength of agreement to each of these questions (2 for Strongly Agree, 1 for Agree, 0 for Disagree). The higher your score the more likely you are to reap all the benefits of nature therapy and become involved in practices that contribute to a healthier planet.[1]

1. I feel at home in the natural world.
2. I enjoy being outdoors.
3. I am sensible but not overly fearful in natural areas.
4. I can appreciate all animals including mammals, insects, fish, reptiles, amphibians, and birds for the role they play in maintaining the cycles of life.
5. I seek out national or state parks, nature preserves, and other relatively untouched areas in which to spend some or all of my weekends and vacations.
6. My interest in the natural world leads me to identify and learn more about the plants and animals in my area.
7. I feel a personal bond with elements of the natural world such as butterflies, trees, and birds.
8. I understand that plants and animals have their own way of knowing and communicating and sensing our presence.
9. The intricacy, power, abilities, and characteristics of natural phenomena inspire my sense of awe and wonder.
10. I know that I come from the same building blocks as the stars and share most of my DNA with other living things. This supports my sense of belonging on earth and bonds with other forms of life.
11. My relationship to nature is an important part of my identity.
12. Natural areas are valuable to human well-being.

13. Natural areas, plants, and wildlife need our protection.
14. My sense of connection to nature and the earth influences my lifestyle.
15. I can influence the health of the natural world through my actions.
16. My well-being is connected to the well-being of the natural world.

NOTE

1. Adapted from Selhub and Logan's *Your Brain on Nature,* 2012, pp. 228–29 and expanded.

References

Abram, D. (2011, November). "The living language," *Shambhala Sun*, 52–58.
Achor, S. (2010). *The happiness advantage: The seven principles of positive psychology that fuel success and performance at work.* New York: Random House.
Amstutz, L. & Mullet, J. (2005). *The little book of restorative justice for schools: Teaching responsibility; creating caring climates.* Intercourse, PA: Good Books.
Ashton-Warner, S. (1963). *Teacher.* New York: Simon & Schuster/Bantam Books.
Barron, C. & Barron, A. (2012). *The creativity cure: A do-it-yourself prescription for happiness.* New York: Scribner.
Ben-Shahar, T. (2007). *Happier: Learn the secrets to daily joy and lasting fulfillment.* New York: McGraw Hill.
Beresford-Kroeger, D. (2010). *The global forest.* New York: Viking.
Beresford-Kroeger, D. (2013). *The sweetness of a simple life: Tips for healthier, happier, and kinder living from the wisdom and science of nature.* Toronto: Random House.
Boorstein, S. (2007). *Happiness is an inside job: Practicing for a joyful life.* New York: Ballantine Books.
Bouvier, R. (1999). "Music in my mother's movement." *Blueberry clouds.* Saskatoon. SK: Thistledown Press.
Burke, L. & Sadler-Smith, E. (2006). "Instructor intuition in the educational setting." *Academy of Management Journal: Teaching and Learning*, 5(2), 169–81.
Burstein, J. (2011). *How creativity works.* New York: Harper.
Caine, G. & Caine, R. (2010). *Strengthening and enriching your professional learning community: The art of learning together.* Alexandria, VA: Association for Supervision and Curriculum Development.
Caldwell, S. (2011). "Simple in means, rich in ends." In A. Johnson & M. Neagly (Eds.), *Educating from the heart: Theoretical and practical approaches to transforming education* (pp. 99–104). Lanham, MD: Rowman & Littlefield Education.
Cervini Manvell, E. (2009). *Teaching is a privilege: Twelve essential understandings for beginning teachers.* Toronto: Rowman & Littlefield Education.

Chade-Meng, T. (2012). *Search inside yourself: The unexpected path to achieving success, happiness (and world peace)*. New York: Harper One.

Richard "Cheech" Marin & Tommy Chong (1970s). *Comedy: Sister Mary Elephant*. Retrieved March 9, 2015 from https://www.youtube.com/watch?v=Aa3HXdqNWIM.

Cheng, F. (2009). *The way of beauty: Five meditations for spiritual transformation*. Rochester, VT: Inner Traditions.

Coleman, M. (2006). *Awake in the wild: Mindfulness in nature as a path of self-discovery*. San Francisco: New World Library.

Cooperrider, D. (1990). "Positive image, positive action: The affirmative basis of organizing." In S. Suresh & D. Cooperrider (Eds.), *Appreciative management and leadership: The power of positive thought and action in organizations* (pp. 91–125). San Francisco: Jossey-Bass.

Cottler, M. (2014). *10 Steps to awakening self-compassion*. Retrieved March 9, 2015 from www.chopra.com/ccl/10-steps-to-awakening-self-compassion.

Csikszentmihalyi, M. (2004). *Flow, the secret to happiness*. [TED Talk]. Retrieved March 9, 2015 from http://www.ted.com/talks/mihaly_csikszentmihalyi_on_flow?language=en.

Curwin, R. & Mendler, A. (1999). *Discipline with dignity*. Alexandria, VA: Association for Supervision and Curriculum Development.

Dalton, J. & Fairchild, L. (2004). *The compassionate classroom: Lessons that nurture wisdom and empathy*. Chicago: Zephyr Press.

De Steno, D. (2014). *The truth about trust: How it determines success in life, love, learning, and more*. New York: Hudson Street.

Dillard, A. (1990). *The writing life*. New York: Harper Perennial.

Dutton, J. (2003). *Energize your workplace: How to create and sustain high-quality connections at work*. San Francisco: Jossey-Bass.

Elias, M. (2012). *Teacher burnout: What are the warning signs?* Retrieved March 9, 2015 from http://www.edutopia.org/blog/teacher-burnout-warning-signs-maurice-elias.

Ferguson, M. (1980). *The Aquarian conspiracy: Personal and social transformation in the 1980s*. Los Angeles: J. P. Tarcher Inc.

Finney, S. (2013). *Strong spirits, kind hearts: Helping students develop inner strength, resilience, and meaning*. Lanham, MD: Rowman & Littlefield Education.

Fischer, N. (2012). *Training in self compassion: Zen teachings on the practice of Lojong*. Boston: Shambhala.

Fitzell, S. (1997). *Free the children! Conflict education for strong and peaceful minds*. Gabriola Island, BC: New Society Publishers.

Fredrickson, B. (2009). *Positivity: Groundbreaking research reveals how to embrace the hidden strength of positive emotions, overcome negativity, and thrive*. New York: Crown Publishers.

Freeman, W. & Scheidecker, D. (2009). *Becoming a legendary teacher: To instruct and inspire*. Thousand Oaks, CA: Corwin.

Gadamer, H-G. (1999). *Truth and method* (2nd ed). (Sheed & Ward Ltd., Trans. 1975; Translation revised by J. Weinsheimer & D. Marshall). New York: Continuum.

Gerecht, H. (1999). *Healing design: Practical Feng Shui for healthy and gracious living*. Boston: Tuttle Publishing.
Germer, C. (2009). *The mindful path to self-compassion: Freeing yourself from destructive thoughts and emotions*. New York: The Guilford Press.
Glasser, W. (1965). *Reality therapy*. New York: Harper & Row Publishers, Inc.
Glazer, S. (Ed.). (1999). *The heart of learning: Spirituality in education*. New York: J. P. Tarcher/Putnam.
Haberman, M. (2004). *Teacher burnout in black & white*. Houston, TX: Haberman Educational Foundation.
Harris, M. (2014). *The end of absence: Reclaiming what we've lost in a world of constant connection*. Toronto: HarperCollins.
Havel, V. (1990). *Disturbing the peace: A conversation with Karel Hvizdala*. New York: Knopf.
Hillman, J. (1983). *Healing fiction*. Woodstock, NY: Spring Publications.
Hoff, B. (1982). *The Tao of Pooh*. Toronto: Penguin Books.
Hogarth, R. (2001). *Educating intuition*. Chicago: University of Chicago Press.
Houston, P. (2011). "Forward: The spirit dimension in education." In A. Johnson & M. Neagley (Eds.), *Educating from the heart: Theoretical and practical approaches to transforming education* (vii–xii). Lanham, MD: Rowman & Littlefield Education.
Hunter, G. (2014). *Life expects: Educating students to lead fulfilling lives*. Domain, MB: The International Centre for Innovation in Education.
Hunter, M. (1997). *Atlantis*. Winnipeg MB: Scirocco Drama/J. Gordon Shillingford Publishing Inc.
Jacobs, G. (2009). *Say good night to insomnia: The 6-week program*. New York: Henry Holt.
Jonas, P. (2009). *Laughing and learning: An alternative to shut up and listen*. Lanham, MD: Rowman & Littlefield Education.
Kabat-Zinn, J. (1990). *Full catastrophe living: Using the wisdom of your body and mind to face stress, pain, and illness*. New York: Delta.
Kabat-Zinn, J. (1994). *Wherever you go, there you are: Mindfulness meditation in everyday life*. New York: Hyperion.
Kabat-Zinn, J. (2005). *Coming to our senses: Healing ourselves and the world through mindfulness*. New York: Hyperion.
Kelm, J. (2008). *The joy of appreciative living: Your 28-day plan to happiness in 3 incredibly easy steps*. New York: Jeremy P. Tarcher.
Kessler, R. (2001). "Soul of students, soul of teachers: Welcoming the inner life to school." In L. Lantieri (Ed.), *Schools with spirit: Nurturing the inner lives of children and teachers* (pp. 107–31). Boston: Beacon Press.
Killinger, B. (2007). *Integrity: Doing the right thing for the right reason*. Montreal and Kingston, ON: McGill-Queens University Press.
Kingwell, M. (2000). *The world we want: Virtue, vice, and the good citizen*. Toronto: Penguin Books.
Kohn, A. (2011). *Feel-bad education: And other contrarian essays on children and schooling*. Boston: Beacon Press.

Kornfield, J. (2008). *The wise heart: A guide to the universal teachings of Buddhist psychology.* New York: Bantam Books.

Kounios, J. & Beeman, M. (2015). *The eureka factor: Aha moments, creative insight, and the brain.* New York: Random House.

Lamott, A. (1994). *Bird by bird: Some instructions on writing and life.* New York: Pantheon Books.

Lantieri, L. (2001). "A Vision of Schools with Spirit." In L. Lantieri (Ed.), *Schools with spirit: Nurturing the inner lives of children and teachers* (pp. 7–20). Boston: Beacon Press.

Larrivee, B. (2012). *Cultivating teacher renewal: Guarding against stress and burnout.* Lanham, MD: Rowman & Littlefield Education.

Lenoir, F. (2015). *Happiness: A philosopher's guide.* Brooklyn, NY: Melville House.

Louv, R. (2005). *Last child in the woods: Saving our children from nature deficit disorder.* Chapel Hill, NC: Alonquin Books of Chapel Hill.

Lundberg, E. & Miller Thurston, C. (2002). *If they're laughing, they just might be listening: Ideas for using humor effectively in the classroom even if you're not funny yourself* (3rd ed.). Fort Collins, CO: Cottonwood.

Lyubomirsky, S. (2008). *The how of happiness: A practical approach to getting the life you want.* New York: Penguin Press.

Lyubomirsky, S. (2013). *The Myths of Happiness: What should make you happy but doesn't, what shouldn't make you happy but does.* New York: Penguin Press.

Maisel, E. (2002). *The Van Gogh blues: The creative person's path through depression.* Navato, CA: New World Library.

Mali, T. (2012). *What teachers make: In praise of the greatest job in the world.* New York: G. P. Putnam's Sons.

Mattis-Namgyel, E. (2010). *The power of the open question: The Buddha's path to freedom.* Boston: Shambhala.

McCarty, M. (2006). *Little big minds: Sharing philosophy with kids.* New York: Jeremy P. Tarcher/Penguin.

McCraty, R., Barrios-Choplin, B., Rozman, D., Atkinson, M., & Watkins, A. (1998). The impact of a new emotional self-management program on stress, emotions, heart rate variability, DHEA and Cortisol." *Integrative Physiological and Behavioural Science,* 33(2), 151–70.

Meyers, D. (2002). *Intuition: Its powers and perils.* New Haven, CT: Yale University Press.

Moore, T. (2008). *A life at work: The joy of discovering what you were born to do.* New York: Broadway Books.

Moore Lappe, F. (1991). *Diet for a small planet: Twentieth anniversary edition.* New York: Ballantine Books.

Nachmanovitch, S. (1990). *Free play: The power of improvisation in life and the arts.* Los Angeles: Jeremy P. Tarcher.

Neff, K. (2013). *Self-compassion step by step: The proven power of being kind to yourself.* Louisville, CO: Sounds True Publishing. (Set of audio CDs.)

Nieto, S. (2003). *What keeps teachers going?* New York: Teachers College Press.

Null, G. (2008). *Living in the moment: A prescription for the soul.* Berkeley, CA: North Atlantic Books.

Odier, D. (2014). *The doors of joy: 19 meditations for authentic living.* London, UK: Watkins Publishing.

Orr, D. (1992). *Ecological literacy: Education and the transition to a postmodern world.* Albany, NY: State University of New York (SUNY) Press.

Palmer, P. (1998). *The Courage to teach: Exploring the inner landscape of the teacher's life.* San Francisco: Jossey-Bass.

Palmer, P. (2000). *Let your life speak: Listening for the voice of vocation.* San Francisco: Jossey-Bass.

Palmer, P. (2001). "Integral life, integral teacher: An interview with Parker J. Palmer." In L. Lantieri (Ed.), *Schools with spirit: Nurturing the inner lives of children and teachers* (pp. 1–6). Boston: Beacon Press.

Palmer, P. with Jackson, M., Jackson, R., & Sluyter, D. (2001). "The Courage to Teach: A Program for Teacher Renewal." In L. Lantieri (Ed.), *Schools with spirit: Nurturing the inner lives of children and teachers* (pp. 132–47). Boston: Beacon Press.

Pennebaker, J. (1997). *Opening up: The healing power of expressing emotion.* New York: Guilford Press.

Peterson, C. & Seligman, M. (2004). *Character strengths and virtues: A handbook and classification.* Washington, DC: American Psychological Association.

Purpel, D. (2004). "A response to the crisis: The love of wisdom and the wisdom of love." In D. Purpel & W. McLaurin, Jr., *Reflections on the moral and spiritual crisis in education* (pp. 261–86). New York: Peter Lang.

Remen, R. (1996). *Kitchen table wisdom: Stories that heal.* New York: Riverhead Books.

Ricard, M. (2015). *Altruism: The power of compassion to change yourself and the world.* (C. Mandell & S. Gordon, Trans.). New York: Little, Brown and Company.

Richards, M. C. (1989). *Centering in pottery, poetry, and the person* (2nd ed.). Middletown, CT: Wesleyan University Press.

Richo, D. (2005). *The five things we cannot change: And the happiness we find by embracing them.* Boston: Shambhala.

Robbins, J. (2012). *The man who planted trees: A story of lost groves, the science of trees, and a plan to save the earth.* New York: Spiegel & Grau.

Robbins, M. (2014). *Nothing changes until you do: A guide to self-compassion and getting out of your own way.* Carlsbad, CA: Hay House, Inc.

Rohr, R. (2011). *Falling upward: A spirituality for the two halves of life.* San Francisco: Jossey-Bass.

Rosenbaum, R. (2013). *Walking the way: 81 Zen encounters with the Tao Te Ching.* Somerville, MA: Wisdom Publications.

Rosenberg, M. (2003). *Nonviolent communication: A language of life* (2nd ed.). Encinitas, CA: Puddle Dancer Press.

Rosenberg, M. (2012). *Living nonviolent communication: Practical tools to connect and communicate skilfully in every situation.* Boulder, CO: Sounds True.

Rowe, S. (2006). *Earth alive: Essays on ecology.* Edmonton, AB: NeWest Press.

Saskatchewan Education. (2001). *Classroom curriculum connections: A teacher's handbook for personal-professional growth.* (S. Finney, writer/developer). Regina SK: Saskatchewan Education.

Schaefer, D. (1996). *The role and nature of aesthetic experience in everyday life.* (Unpublished master's thesis). Regina, SK: University of Regina.

Schoeberlein, D. with Seth, S. (2009). *Mindful teaching and teaching mindfulness: A guide for anyone who teaches anything.* Somerville, MA: Wisdom Publications.

Schön, D. (1983). *The reflective practitioner: How professionals think in action.* New York: Basic Books.

Selhub, E. & Logan, A. (2012). *Your brain on nature: The science of nature's influence on your health, happiness, and vitality.* Mississauga, ON: Wiley.

Seigel, D. & Hartzell, M. (2003). *Parenting from the inside out: How a deeper self-understanding can help you raise children who thrive.* New York: Jeremy P. Tarcher/Penguin.

Seligman, M. (2011). *Flourish: A visionary new understanding of happiness and well-being.* New York: Free Press.

Seligman, M., Steen, T., Park, N. & Peterson, C. (2005). "Positive psychology progress: Empirical validations of interventions." *American Psychologist,* 60, 410–21.

Shapiro, S. & Skinulis, K. (2000). *Classrooms that work: A teacher's guide to discipline without stress.* Richmond Hill, ON: Practical Parenting Program.

Showkeir, J. & Showkeir, M. (2008). *Authentic Conversations: Moving from manipulation to truth and commitment.* San Francisco: BK Publishers.

Solnit, R. (2013). *The faraway nearby.* New York: Viking.

Spretnak, C. (1991). *States of grace: The recovery of meaning in the postmodern age.* San Francisco: HarperCollins.

Stone Zander, R. & Zander, B. (2000). *The art of possibility.* New York: Penguin Books.

Stronge, J., Tucker, P. & Hindman, J. (2004). *Handbook for qualities of effective teachers.* Alexandria, VA: ASCD.

Suzuki, D. (2007). *The sacred balance: Rediscovering our place in nature.* Vancouver: The David Suzuki Foundation/Greystone Books.

Swimme, B. (2001). *The universe is a green dragon: A cosmic creation story.* Rochester, VT: Bear & Company.

Thurgood Sagal, J. (2009). *Shifting horizons of understanding: How teachers interpret curriculum in their practice.* Saarbrücken: VDM Verlag.

Vanslyke-Briggs, K. (2010). *The nurturing teacher: Managing the stress of caring.* Toronto: Rowman & Littlefield Education.

Warren, D. (2010). *Cool water: A novel.* Toronto: HarperCollins.

Wells, G. (1986). *The meaning makers: Children learning language and using language to learn.* Portsmouth, NH: Heinemann.

Westman, M. (2001). "Stress and strain crossover." *Human Relations,* 54, 717–51.

Wimberger, L. (2014). *Neurosculpting for stress relief: Practices to change your brain and your life.* Louisville, CO: Sounds True Publishing. (Set of two CDs.)

Winter, K. (2014). *Boundless: Tracing land and dream in a new Northwest Passage.* Toronto: House of Anansi Press.

About the Authors

Sandra Finney, PhD, has had many roles in her lifetime in education, including that of public school teacher, curriculum developer, and teacher educator – at all times working to support the overall well-being, compassion, ecological values, and critical and creative thinking abilities of teachers and students. She is the author of *Strong Spirits, Kind Hearts: Helping Students Develop Inner Strength, Resilience, and Meaning.*

Jane Thurgood Sagal, EdD, has served as a teacher, educational administrator, and curriculum leader in the K–12 education sector for more than thirty-four years. In her previous publication, *Shifting Horizons of Understanding: How Teachers Interpret Curriculum in Their Practice,* she demonstrates her commitment to collaborative engagement with others and the inclusion of a diversity of voices in her work.

CPSIA information can be obtained
at www.ICGtesting.com
Printed in the USA
LVHW090509181119
637660LV00001B/18/P